C000146691

Max Boyce grew u[...] left school at fiftee[...] is from the warmth and humour of that community that he draws the inspiration for his songs and verse. From the mid-seventies his albums have sold in millions, winning him several gold discs, and his earlier book of poems, stories and songs, *I Was There* was an instant bestseller.

MAX BOYCE IN

THE MAD PURSUIT OF APPLAUSE

HEADLINE

First published in Great Britain in 1987
by Pavilion Books Limited,
in association with Michael Joseph Limited

First published in paperback in 1988
by HEADLINE BOOK PUBLISHING PLC

ISBN 0 7472 3167 2

Printed and bound in Great Britain by
Collins, Glasgow

HEADLINE BOOK PUBLISHING PLC
Headline House
79 Great Titchfield Street
London W1P 7FN

Contents

To Cathy and Rhiannon. For the times I went away.

Introduction

*T*here is a certain romanticism about being 'on tour'. It is a way of life that can only be glimpsed by those who have not been 'on the road'.

It is true that the balladeer with his fiddle and banjo has long since been replaced by a ten-ton truck, mixing deck and graphic equaliser, but we performers are still essentially travelling people, selling our stories and songs to those who might listen.

It is an unnatural world, inhabited largely by Indian waiters and night porters (who only have bottles), and where the only gourmet delights after a long night are Chinese takeaways.

It is here where a 'do not disturb' sign takes on a whole new meaning when the silence of that early morning world is shattered by 'sorry I'll call back again' chambermaids whose sole role in life is to drive trolleys of shampoo sachets, green soap and towels clattering down corridors shouting above the vacuum cleaner, 'Muriel! Will you do 56 and 12, love?' When they are sure everyone and everything is awake, they disappear into broom cupboards, never to be seen again.

It is in these cupboards that the shampoo sachets are kept. These are made of a special indestructible material which can only be torn apart by the teeth at precisely that moment when the shower suddenly goes cold. You, anyway, usually manage to swallow the entire contents of the sachet!

Still, this is all part of being 'on the road'. It is a tiring, wearying and unhealthy occupation, but it is what I know and enjoy most of all.

It is even more exhausting in strange and distant lands, where the language barrier adds to the confusion.

I remember being in Hong Kong and ringing the front desk to complain that my air conditioning wasn't working. Two hours later there came a knock on my door and an immaculately dressed Chinese boy appeared with a bottle of Pears shampoo. I enquired, 'What's this?' He answered, 'You ask for air conditioner . . .'

This book is a collection of some of my experiences. I hope you enjoy my travels and share in the laughter and heartbreak of being 'on the road' – all in the mad pursuit of applause.

Safe journey,
Max Boyce

Fear of Flying

*I*n my early days, the fear of flying took the edge off any overseas tours. Thankfully I no longer need Valium or brandy and have overcome the fear of flying . . . it's only the crashing that bothers me now . . .

I have always wondered why the aviation authorities don't make aeroplanes out of the same material as they use for the 'black box'.

One thing that reinforces my fear of flying is that you never see an *old* stewardess.

I was put off flying by my first flight. It was to Shannon from Swansea Airport. It was an extremely cheap flight and on an airline I had not heard of . . . and haven't since.

Our journey was fraught with problems from the moment we arrived at the airport. On checking in we were told the aircraft would be an hour late in arriving from Shannon. We naturally enquired why, and were told – it had been crop spraying . . .

When it did arrive, it looked like something out of an airfix kit, with the wings coloured by the 'Paint with Numbers' system.

However, it did take off, albeit rather noisily. When the seat belt sign had been switched off, the captain (who was seen wearing a St Christopher) spoke over the intercom: 'Hello, this is your captain speaking. Welcome aboard flight ZL Zero 436 from Swansea to Shannon. We are now cruising at an altitude of twelve thousand feet, but in a few minutes we will be landing at Swindon to take on some more wood.'

In the Land of the Long White Cloud

*O*ne of the places I looked forward most to visiting was New Zealand, because of the great rugby rivalry which exists between Wales and the 'Land of the Long White Cloud'.

My tour began with a concert in Auckland, and I desperately wanted to do well. I began by telling them the 'true' story of what happened in 1971 when, during the British Lions tour, a challenge was thrown out by a local businessman to see if any man could walk across the waters of Lake Taratoa.

Three men entered. From New Zealand – the legendary All Black forward Colin Meads. From Wales – the equally famous Gareth Edwards. And – the Pope . . .

The first to venture across was Gareth. The New Zealand crowd who were watching started to sing, 'Now is the hour for us to say goodbye . . .' – while the watching Welsh supporters sang, 'Guide him O Thou great Jehovah . . .'

Gareth walked across and walked back, as did Colin Meads.

Then came the turn of the Pope. He went half-way, lost his concentration, and in he went – splosh.

Colin Meads turned to Gareth and said, 'You're one hell of a boy, Gareth – not telling him about the stepping stones.'

And Gareth said, 'What stepping stones?'

Everywhere I went in New Zealand, people kept asking me how seriously we took our rugby football in Wales.

I tried to explain that our love of rugby was really a manifestation of nationhood, and simplified it somewhat by telling them the 'true' story of how before one rugby international at Twickenham, I found myself without a ticket and then luckily – at the last minute – my uncle died.

Unfortunately the funeral was arranged the same day and time as the game. I couldn't go to both so I went to Twickenham.

When we came back on the Thursday I asked how the funeral had gone.

'Oh Max,' they said, 'it was a disaster.'

'What happened?'

'We were gathered around the graveside, we had just sung the 23rd Psalm and there was this gravedigger listening to the match on a transistor radio. When the result came through from Twickenham – England 9, Wales 8 – he told the chap next to him the score, and he told the chap next to him . . .

'Before long everybody in the funeral party knew the score – the bearer, the wreaths, the family, the friends. And do you know,' he said, 'it cast a gloom over the whole proceedings . . .'

One of the most unforgettable moments on that tour came at Ponsonby Rugby Club in Auckland, when our hosts were a Mr and Mrs Bowden. I had said in passing that I regretted not having enough time to visit Rotorua to hear some traditional Maori singing. Our hosts, anxious to please us in every way, approached some Maoris. They were gathered around a big table drinking huge quantities of beer out of enamel jugs.

One of them, who weighed at least thirty stone and apparently was some sort of prince, said something in Maori. They immediately without question drew together, and after one had sung out they all joined in – all in superb controlled close harmony. It was totally unrehearsed and quite beautiful and something I will never forget.

When we were asked to reply in kind, John Neil and I tried valiantly with a traditional Welsh folk song, 'Ar Lan Y Môr' (By the Sea Shore), but we paled in comparison with the unique sound of those South Sea Islanders . . .

While I was in New Zealand I came face to face with Brian McKechnie, the All Black full-back who kicked a controversial penalty against Wales at Cardiff in 1978. His kick, which followed the Andy Haden dying swan routine, had denied Wales a famous and long overdue victory over the All Blacks. It was undoubtedly the most disappointing moment I have ever experienced in watching or playing sport.

Brian was a quiet, gentle person whom I liked instantly. I explained to him that it wasn't the losing that upset me, it was the BBC . . . They kept showing it. I realise they had to show it once or twice, but what I will never forgive them for is showing it in *slow motion* . . .

It was shown live in *Grandstand*, and repeated on the *Six O'Clock News* (from several camera angles) and then again on *Rugby Special* with Nigel Starmer-Smith on BBC2 the same night.

Watching it yet again on BBC Wales television on Sunday afternoon I had my own back. I watched, knowing every gesture and movement as Brian placed the ball and began his run. Little did he know this, but as he swung his leg back I ran behind the set, adjusted the 'vertical hold' and shifted the posts over six inches.

I told this story 'in concert' in Auckland, and Terry McLean, the famous New Zealand rugby writer and fibre-tipped assassin, wrote in his review of my concert (albeit tongue in cheek): 'For the first time I found to my utter dismay a liking for a Welshman . . .'

Some weeks later we met again, and I in turn, much to my dismay, found a liking for him.

When I was in New Zealand it gladdened my heart to hear

people talk with deep affection of Wales and of the welcome they had received there from the people they had met.

It was good to meet up with old friends at Ponsonby Rugby Club in Auckland and, as is common in rugby the world over, we turned night into day and exchanged addresses, stories and ties.

I told them the story of how before the Centenary Test against New Zealand at Cardiff, in 1978, I had arranged to meet my old friend Billy Williams outside the Angel Hotel before the game. He had managed to get us two stand tickets on the half-way line, and I looked forward immensely to the confrontation with the All Blacks.

We had a few drinks in the bar, rekindling a hundred friendships and savouring the unique atmosphere and excitement of Cardiff on International day. The songs came on a tray, and 'Calon Lân' and 'Cwm Rhondda' rang from every bar, whilst some New Zealand supporters enacted a Maori War dance in the foyer. Lipstick and eyeshadow sufficed as warpaint, whilst an oil painting of the Marquis of Bute was borrowed as a shield.

This was greeted with wild applause only to be followed by a man from Cross Hands in Dyfed who played the piano whilst holding two oranges. This was received with even greater acclaim, and he was given a booking at Ferndale Band Club.

It was now time to make our way to the ground. We pushed our way through the milling crowd that thronged Westgate Street, sympathising with the pleading cries of the 'ticketless' lined up along the 'wailing' wall: 'Any spares? Any spares?'

As we approached the great ornate Gwyn Nichols gates, we could hear the crowd inside the ground cheering and singing. My heart leapt and I thrilled with eager anticipation.

Bill turned to me and said, 'I wish I had my piano here.'

'Why?' I laughed, 'So you could lead the crowd in song?'

'No,' he replied sadly. 'Our tickets are on it . . .'

Bill and I went to drown our (and several other people's) sorrows and returned home in the wee small hours a little the worse for wear. Next morning I awoke with a terrible hangover. My little girl crawled into bed beside me and said gently but firmly, 'Don't wear that red and white scarf again, Daddy – it always gives you a bad head . . .'

I enjoyed my time in the Land of the Long White Cloud, as the Maoris call it, and to those who believe the New Zealander lacks a sense of humour, I suggest they read the sign in Auckland Airport's departure lounge, which bears the following request: 'Will the last person leaving New Zealand please put the lights out.'

Canadian Peking Duck

We were in Canada for a concert at the huge O'Keefe Centre in Toronto, which seats 3,500. The day before we were advised to visit a particular Chinese restaurant called The Champion House in Toronto's Chinatown.

Apparently, it was very famous and had been featured extensively in magazines and good food guides. It had the added attraction of white walls and ceilings that were covered with writings and drawings by customers praising the restaurant.

We ordered Peking Duck, which evidently was the speciality of the house. On receipt of our order a little waiter struck a huge Chinese gong and shouted into the kitchen, 'Peking Duck, Peking Duck.'

We ordered some wine and eagerly awaited our meal.

Some forty-five minutes later (it takes a while) the gong was sounded once more – 'Peking Duck' – and this little stir-fried Chinese waiter appeared from the kitchen with a huge cooked duck on a silver salver. The duck was still replete with neck, beak and paddles. The waiter then produced a cleaver and motioned to me, 'You cut head off.'

'No! No! I couldn't possibly,' I replied.

My colleague Bill Thomson remonstrated with me. 'Max, it's probably an old Chinese custom dating back to the Ming Dynasty. They'll be offended if you don't do as they ask.'

'I don't care, Bill. I just can't do it.'

'Give it here!' snapped Bill, and performed the necessary act as I looked away.

We were then served with several different dishes made from the duck. The prime delicacy was the crispy skin served with mandarin pancakes, shallots, shredded cucumber and plum sauce, and we finished with a soup made from the duck's bones.

The meal was quite superb, and I told the little waiter so, finished my wine and we prepared to leave, leaving a few Canadian dollars for the waiter.

He bowed politely, thanked me and then produced a felt-tip pen and invited me to write suitable comments on the wall.

Suitably mellowed by then, I clambered on to the table and wondered what to write. I thought for a while and then wrote slowly and meaningfully: 'My duck was so good it could have played rugby for Wales' – and signed it with a flourish.

The little Chinaman blinked and asked me, 'What you lite?'

I explained, reading it out aloud for him, 'My duck was so good . . .'

He looked at me, hard and long.

'I no understand what you lite – lugby?'

I tried then hopelessly amongst hysterical laughter from our table and some customers nearby to explain, only to get him more confused. I thought of their equivalent and started again.

'If I was Chinese . . .'

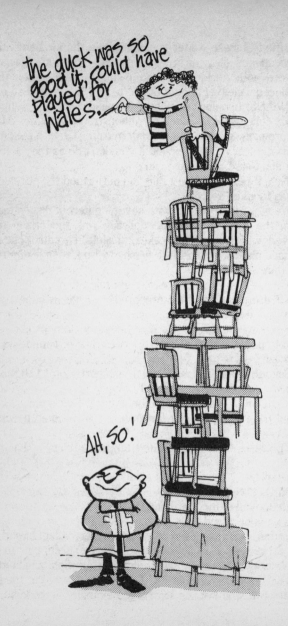

18

'You Chinese?' he asked, astonished.

'No! No! You're not listening. *If* I was Chinese – I would have written – "My duck was so good it could have played *Ping Pong* for China."'

He stared long and then said, 'Ah, no can, not possible.'

'Why?' I asked.

He shook his head and pointed to Bill, 'He cut head off!'

Kitchen Cloths and Fan Belts

The problems associated with touring the Middle East are many and varied. Ours started at the International Airport in Bahrain, when one of the band was refused permission to enter the country because he had an Israeli work permit stamped in his passport. Eventually, after much delicate diplomacy, we were allowed entry and made our way into the city.

When we arrived in the hotel, Neil Lewis, my long-serving musician, telephoned home. His mother naturally enquired what it was like in the Middle East.

'It's very hot,' said Neil. 'It's 130 degrees in the shade!'

'Then I'd stay out of the shade if I were you,' replied Mrs Lewis.

The hotel was very modern, and as it was only just over a week to Christmas they had a special display in the foyer. There were three life-size cardboard angels with wire haloes, paper wings and the sheet music of 'Silent Night' on a stand in front of them.

We walked around Bahrain in the afternoon. Much of it resembled a building site, and I couldn't get over the squalor of some of the houses with the inevitable air conditioner

19

cassetted into the breeze blocked walls. There would invariably be a big Mercedes parked outside. I wondered why they didn't live in their cars and drive their houses around.

We did all the tourist spots and had our photos taken with a moth-eaten camel who spat at everybody. Apparently the camels are something of a problem at night as they wander on to the roads, in the same way as sheep on the Heads of the Valley motorway. In the night the sand becomes very cold, so the camels seek the warm road surfaces that have retained the heat of the day. This inevitably leads to accidents. If you are unlucky enough to hit a camel and kill it you are expected to pay for it, and if the camel is pregnant you are expected to pay for two camels. To this day, every camel that has been knocked down has been pregnant . . .

It had been apparent even at the airport that Arab customs and culture affect everyone, none more so than the thousands of British ex-pats who work and live in the Middle East. I was astonished to find at the airport that every British newspaper had been 'censored'. There was an Arab leafing through the British newspapers on the look-out for scantily clad girls. The *Sun* came in for special attention. He would turn to page three and with a felt-tip pen cover over the topless model's nipples. (One of the band suggested it was a job for two men – the second to come around every twenty minutes with a bucket of cold water.) I couldn't help but wonder what the person employed to do this work put on his passport to describe his occupation . . . Nippler?!

Even the hotel magazines' underwear advertisements were defiled in the same way, some even going so far as 'nippling out' babies in rusk and nappy adverts.

I fully intended to use this priceless material in the forthcoming concerts and wondered how many, if any, 'locals' would attend. The tour promoter, Bill Thomson, an ebullient, over-efficient, worrying and wonderful man, who had great experience of working in the Middle East, begged me not to mention any of these 'sensitive areas', and on no

20

account was I to describe the Bahrain Arab traditional dress as 'nightgowns with kitchen cloths and fan belts'.

He also urged me to stay clear of religion, as the son of one of the rulers was coming to the concert, and any displeasure on his part could result in our being thrown into hessian bags and stoned in the marketplace.

I decided to consult some of the staff in the hotel as to the possible reaction if I did mention certain religious aspects and made humorous observations about the traditional way of life in the Middle East. I asked one waiter if he would be personally offended. He said, 'I am not caring a . . . I am from Bombay.'

Most of the waiters in the hotel were Indian and they kept coming up and asking me could they hold my leek.

'Mr Mac,' said one. 'Can I please be having my photo with you and your onion? I am wanting to send it to my sister in Birmingham. You and Iron Bottom [Ian Botham] are her favourites.'

The Indians were so gentle and friendly and without exception were all terrified of Bill. He maintained, 'They don't listen,' and much to our amusement they continued to infuriate him.

Bill asked one Indian driver at the airport if he knew the British Club in Bahrain and could he take us there. He replied, 'Oh! Yes I am knowing it.'

'Are you sure you know it?' asked Bill, having had a catalogue of previous disasters.

The young Indian driver was indignant, and cried 'Why are you asking me again? I have already told you – I *am* knowing it.'

The band loaded all the gear into a hired truck, and Bill told the taxi driver we'd follow him to the British Club and not to go too fast. He looked at Bill and said, 'But I am not knowing where it is.'

Bill exploded 'What!!! – I asked you *twice* and you said you knew the British Club.'

'That is correct, Mr Thomson. I *am* knowing it, but I am not knowing where it is.'

I hugged the little driver, and Bill went off ranting and raving, 'They don't listen . . . They just don't . . .'

We eventually reached the club, where we were told the concert was a sell-out. I was understandably thrilled, especially as it was our first tour in the Middle East. The sales had been reinforced by rugby club parties who had chartered planes from Saudi and from Dubai. We ended up with an estimated audience of 1,500, seated outdoors around the hotel swimming pool. A special stage with lighting had been built, and a PA system installed.

I waited to make my entrance in my thick red coat, long trailing scarf and my much-travelled leek. The only way to get on stage without being seen by the audience was through the hotel's kitchen. I felt a little self-conscious waiting there as the chefs and the waiters giggled and pointed. In my stage get-up the heat of the kitchen was almost unbearable. I couldn't help but think of the old adage, which had come true: 'If you can't stand the heat – get out of the kitchen.'

I was soaked through with perspiration when Neil, after what seemed like an age, announced, 'There's nothing more to say except . . .' (Drumroll) 'Will you please give a big warm welcome to . . . Max Boyce!'

We were given a tremendous welcome and the concert was a huge success. I had thought the rugby lads who had flown in would be hard to control, especially as they'd been drinking heavily hours before the concert got under way, but my fears were unfounded. They were wildly enthusiastic throughout the whole concert and were genuinely thrilled we had come to the Middle East.

I asked some of them afterwards how they had adjusted to life in the Middle East. One lad from Newcastle, who had flown in from Sharjah, explained: 'The drink's no problem – we can get it, anyway – even in Saudi – as long as you drink it in the privacy of your own home and . . . you don't get caught. The one thing I do miss is women. When you've been here a while, Max, you start looking at camels and thinking – "Haven't they got long eyelashes?"'

The night wore on and the swimming pool by now was completely covered in empty beer cans. To the strains of 'Round and round went the bloody big wheel', the trainer of one rugby club was made to walk a crudely fashioned plank. Several of his team-mates stripped off to dive in, and sank him while a six-foot shark (the entertainments secretary with a cardboard fin) attempted to swallow his juicier parts.

The Arabs who had come to the concert laughed hysterically, and only one as far as I know rummaged in his handbag for a felt-tip pen . . .

On the way to bed, I wished some Arabs 'Good Night, God Bless' – to which one smiled and said, 'We do not recognise your God.'

I slept soundly that night, only to be wakened by the ritual early morning prayers. From my fourth floor room I heard a devout Moslem wailing the early prayers with the aid of a public address system strapped to his back, ensuring that no one in the city slept.

I rose and looked out of my window. The swimming pool was still littered with empty beer cans, and there, floating in the shallow end, were the head of a smiling angel and a damp copy of 'Silent Night'.

Some months later I met the Food and Beverages Manager of the hotel in London. I thanked him once again for his kindness and for looking after us so well, and apologised for the fact that one of his angels had been manhandled. I explained it had only been high spirits and that the lads had tried to repair it. He laughed and said, 'It's all right, Max, they cancelled Christmas anyway!'

Apparently, a few days before the 25th of December the Ruler decided there would be no Christmas. There were to be no celebrations. All festivities were to cease . . . He cancelled Christmas.

*L*ittle did I know what I was letting myself in for when I agreed to take part in a film about 'gridiron' football in America.

It followed Jasper Carrott's hilarious film by the same company, Opix Films, about his experience with an American soccer team called the Tampa Bay Rowdies.

The team we were to involve ourselves with was the Dallas Cowboys.

This was a few years before the sport had gained popularity in Great Britain, and the film was designed to explain, inform and generally whet the appetite of the new Channel 4 public.

I freely admit that at the time the Dallas Cowboys meant little to me, but the prospect of studying and getting to know the game in America intrigued me.

Such is the thoroughness of the Cowboys' system that before they agreed to the making of the film they wanted to establish my suitability. The Vice Chairman of the Dallas Cowboys, a Mr Joe Bailey, came to London and a lunch meeting was arranged. We talked and, loosened up by a few beers, shared a few stories.

I ended up much later learning a gridiron move or 'play'

called *Blue Toss 39 Right on Two* which resulted in me 'rushing' eighty-five yards (after an interception outside Fenwicks) for a touch-down at the junction of Carlisle Street and Dean Street. Joe kicked the extra point.

Suitably impressed by my balanced running *and* my knowledge of real ale, he declared me suitable.

Later that week I met Gareth Edwards following the England–Wales rugby international at Twickenham. I mentioned that I was going to Dallas to have a look at American football and that I was desperately keen.

'Well, whatever you do, Max,' Gareth insisted, 'don't get involved.'

'But what if I train hard and lose weight?' I argued.

'You'll get killed.'

'But what if I take steroids?'

'They'll walk all over you.'

'But what if I paint a dragon on my helmet?'

'Ah!' said Gareth, weighing it up. 'That's different.'

I laughed and he wished me well.

Dallas

Thus forewarned, the next week we flew into Dallas. I was interviewed on arrival by a local film crew, and in my eagerness to please, sang them a little ditty with a suitable Southern drawl.

We flew into Dallas and I tell you all so far
I ain't seen Miss Ellie yet and I sure ain't seen J.R.
And I ain't been to Southfork, the ranch that's on TV,
But I'm with the Dallas Cowboys and that's good enough for
   me.

They said I was 'kinda cute' and then enquired what position I was going to play.

I hadn't appreciated that the producer – because of his enthusiasm for the project – had omitted to tell them I had never seen, let alone played, American football. I wondered why many of them stared at me and slowly shook their heads.

They had understood that I was a well-known name in British rugby, but no one had told them in what capacity.

I kept hearing whispered conversations, and comments like 'He's kinda small, ain't he?'

After a few days' acclimatisation in Dallas I was asked to undertake a searching medical examination, including the delicate question of possible impotency. Apparently, this was not uncommon amongst gridiron players following long and rigorous weight training schedules.

After the medical, I was asked to go on a fifteen-mile run so that doctors could ascertain my physical condition on return.

When I did *eventually* return, my face like a red pepper, everyone had left the building, the place was in darkness and I was presumed lost . . .

The next day I was introduced to one of the coaches and given my play-book, the 'bible' of the gridiron player, where every set move or 'play' of the side was listed and diagramatically drawn. There were over 250 of these so-called 'plays', each of which had to be memorised perfectly.

Some of them were fairly straightforward, but others were incredibly complex and resembled a knitting pattern. I shuddered at the thought of playing a vitally important match, a 'play' being called by the quarter-back, and finding myself having to ask which one it was. I resolved I would learn as many as I could, and that night I went to sleep with the 'bible' by my bed.

Maybe I Ain't Big Enough

After a few days in Dallas, which I found to be one of the friendliest places I have ever been and totally unlike its television image, we flew to the Dallas Cowboys' training camp in California.

The reason the training camp was in California, some thousand miles away, was because the intense heat in Texas at that time of the year made it quite unbearable.

The training camp used by the Cowboys was a college campus in the foothills of the mountains at a place called Thousand Oaks, some thirty miles north of Los Angeles.

I shall never forget that first morning being introduced as an *athlete*-cum-entertainer from *England* who was going to try out for the Cowboys.

I looked around at these huge men with some apprehension and wondered, 'What am I doing here?'

One of them approached me and said, 'You're kinda small to be in the trenches, ain't ya?'

I said, 'I haven't been very well . . . !'

He just smiled and said, 'You're gonna get worse . . .'

I was then taken to the kit room by a friendly Texan known as 'Cotton' because of his straw-coloured hair.

Unlike in most games, each player is allocated a number, and mine was to be ten, which I was thrilled about. I explained with boyish exuberance that this number had a special significance in Wales, being the number worn by the outside-half in rugby, and that we had a great tradition of them with players like Cliff Morgan, Phil Bennett, Barry John, etc.

They looked blankly at me and obviously hadn't heard of any of the people I had mentioned – in fact knew virtually nothing about rugby football.

'Tell me, Max,' one asked. 'Why is it that people who play rugby haven't got any teeth?'

I answered, 'It's to stop them biting each other.'

He looked at me astonished. 'You don't say.'

They were without exception in total awe of rugby football, and kept saying they wouldn't dream of playing it.

'Those guys don't wear any pads.'

I was then given all the necessary protection, the huge shoulder pads, forearm pads, thigh pads, knee guards and my helmet. It had three or four steel bars forming a grille across the front, which I thought would have made it impossible to catch the ball or even to see it properly.

They explained it was a 'linebacker's' helmet (gridiron's equivalent of a front-row forward in rugby) and in that position the ball was purely incidental. I found it quite astonishing to be told that linebackers could go several seasons without handling the ball at all.

For my first few days I was to be part of the defensive line-up and to find out what it was like to be 'in the trenches'.

The first thing I was shown was a helmet slap, which in effect was a legal short-arm tackle delivered with the extended forearm to the side of the head.

I foolishly asked this huge player, a man of Irish extraction called 'Fitzy', to illustrate this. I was keen to know what degree of protection the helmet afforded. He chuckled, shrugged his shoulders and hit me clean over a bench into one of the changing lockers.

The film director shouted excitedly, 'Great! Great! Can we do that again on a wide angle . . . ?!!!'

Fitzy helped me out of the locker and enquired, 'You OK?'

He appeared slightly out of focus, but naturally I insisted that it hadn't hurt at all and that I was looking forward to playing 'in the trenches'!

Before each training session every player was taken to be weighed and strapped up. Every joint was strapped with tape to minimise the chance of injury. After my experience in the dressing-room, I was quite relieved to hear this and ended up some twenty minutes later resembling something from an Egyptian tomb. This, coupled with all the protective gear, made movement very restricted but after my flirtation with the locker I was quite prepared to put up with any discomfort.

This was the first time I had seen the rest of the 'rookies' – the other new players who were at the training camp hoping to become 'Dallas Cowboys'. There were some forty to fifty of these rookies, who had been 'drafted' from colleges all over America after being watched in college games by the network of Cowboy scouts that covered the whole country.

I found the method of drafting players fascinating. Apparently the side that finishes in bottom position in the league is given the first choice of new college players in the following season. The team finishing in first position in, say, a league of ten would be given the tenth choice, and then it's the turn of the side finishing last to choose their second player, and so on. This process is repeated until forty or so college players have been selected by each professional side.

This seemed a very democratic system and was similar to the way we chose teams as youngsters in the park or the school yard. There two captains were picked, a coin was tossed and whoever won had the choice of the best player.

Despite the undoubted fairness of this method of selection, it seemed to me a little harsh on the individual player's freedom of choice. I was also astonished to discover that, out of the forty or so college players selected by the Dallas Cowboys, only three or four on average would be retained at the end of the six weeks at training camp. They would then go on to become professional footballers with the Dallas Cowboys.

This, for many of the rookies, was to be the most important few weeks of their lives. For the established players, or 'veterans' as they were known, these rookies represented a threat to their place in the team.

Each morning would start with breakfast around eight o'clock and then we would be weighed and strapped up. Any player sustaining an injury through not having been strapped would automatically be fined. The morning session lasted from nine until twelve, and after lunch, vitamin pills and salt tablets there was a further afternoon session from two until around five. This was followed by a sort of night school from seven until nine, involving talks and lectures.

There was very little, if any, of the beer drinking associated with rugby football, and in fact most players were glad to be in bed by ten o'clock. However, coaches were sent around our 'dormitories' at ten to check if indeed we were 'home'. Any 'vet' not answering his late night call would be fined. There were occasions when some of the vets (whose place in the team was assured) never came 'home' at all and during the evening class of the next day were fined very heavily and subsequently disciplined (much to the joy of the rest of the squad).

In these evening classes I found it almost impossible to stay awake, not because I wasn't interested; I was so desperately tired.

Maybe I Ain't Good Enough

The training schedule was carried out six days a week and subsequently I found myself absolutely shattered attempting to keep up with the other rookies, who were so much younger, fitter and stronger. They, meanwhile, came to look on me as something of an oddity, especially as a linebacker.

After the first week they had me lined up in a confrontation with Ed 'Too Tall' Jones, the biggest man I had ever seen, standing some six foot ten and built like a brick 'public convenience'. He was a living legend in American football, and was part of the Dallas Cowboys' famed and much feared 'Doomsday Defence'.

The coach rubbed me down, and whispered the play call 'on two'. This enabled me beforehand to know when to move. He would call some play like 'Delta Green Shotgun 85, 25 – Hut! Hut!'

The second time he called 'Hut' would be the signal for me to strike (i.e. on two). This is done in a game in an attempt to lure the opposition offside.

The coach said to me, 'Number Ten, I want you to walk all over him, hit him in the numbers, chew him up and spit him out!'

We went down into what American footballers call a three-point stance, a crouched position with one finger of one hand touching the ground, ready to spring forward. We were barely a yard apart. The other rookies looked on, whooping in delight and shouting encouragement.

'Go get him, Max. Haul his ass!'

The coach whispered, 'OK Number Ten, you ready?'

'Yeah,' I snarled, trying to look mean.

'Delta Green Shotgun 85, 25 – Hut! Hut! . . .'

I leapt at 'Too Tall' screaming, totally committed and determined to knock him over. He stopped me with one piston-like hand, picked me up above his head like a child – and dropped me to the ground in a heap. I picked my crumpled body up with tears in my eyes. The coach could hardly stop himself from laughing.

'What happened, Number Ten?'

'I slipped,' I said.

'Number Ten,' he went on. 'You're the waste of a good helmet! You're too old, too slow and too small.'

'Don't mess about, coach,' I replied. 'Give it to me straight!'

'You just ain't gonna make it with us. You better try somewhere else.'

I slunk away, shouting back to him in a choked voice, 'You wait 'til I paint a dragon on my helmet . . . !'

I lay awake that night and wrote some words to a song:

> Now I know this game is hard and rough,
> And maybe I ain't big enough,
> And maybe my best days are gone,
> But I'm the kind of guy who ain't afraid to try,
> Even if I die – with my boots on . . . !

In those first couple of days a few other rookies were discarded, or 'cut', and this would be the pattern at the end of each week until the squad was whittled right down. Those who had not impressed or reached the necessary standard were informed, 'Mr Landry would like to see you, bring your play-book.'

Mr Landry was the head coach, and arguably the most famous in America. He was always dressed in a sombre suit and a trilby hat, and never smiled. These rookies were taken to see him and it was explained to them why they had been cut. They then just simply packed their things and returned home.

For those boys, who had set their hearts on becoming pro footballers with the Cowboys, this was a traumatic experience and reduced many of them to tears. Some were cut only days before the end of training camp. To these players who had so nearly made it, it was particularly distressing, and I felt desperately sorry for them.

What I found astonishing was the fact that those who had failed to make it just returned to normal occupations and never ever played football again. Gridiron football after college is a professional game, and there just aren't any amateur teams. If you make it you stand the chance of fame and fortune. If you don't, it's back to relative obscurity.

This threat hanging over the rookies destroyed some players while bringing out a steely strength in some other less gifted ones. It also created a bond between us, which invariably happens in shared adversity, and I was thrilled to hear the other rookies pick up a simple little song of resolve I had written. The chorus of which went:

> All the rookies sing this song,
> We're gonna sing it all night long.
> We don't wanna get Cut! Cut! Cut!,
> We just wanna go Hut! Hut! Hut!

After my ordeal in the trenches I was relieved to hear that the following week I was to try out in a position called 'punt receiver'. This specialised position required the ability to catch unerringly the high ball following a kick-off (and run until you're flattened . . .).

I was fairly optimistic I would be able to acquit myself reasonably in this position, as it required no great strength or size. I had never been a great rugby player, but I had always possessed a safe pair of hands, whether it was at full-back or patrolling the long-leg boundary in cricket. After my disastrous first few days I looked forward to this new challenge.

The second week of training camp saw the arrival of more of the established players, and the crowd watching the training sessions grew to well over a thousand.

I was introduced to the punt receiver coach (each position had its own coach) who was to gauge my potential. I was taken to an area near the crowd and showed this contraption, a machine which resembled a cannon and was used to simulate a high kick. The ball was thrust down the snout of the barrel of this cannon and fired towards the waiting catcher or punt receiver.

There were certain adjustments that could be made to the machine that altered the ball's flight, height and range, thus making it more or less difficult for the catcher.

I watched them operate this machine and marvelled as my fellow punt receivers caught everything the cannon fired at them, equipped as they were with the special open face or single grille helmet.

It then came to my turn . . .

Because it was being filmed, and because of the cannon operator's inane sense of humour, he adjusted the machine so that there was maximum height and velocity and also ensured that it would spin in flight.

I stood waiting nervously some forty yards away, squinting through the grille of my linebacker's helmet. I prepared myself mentally and loosened up with a few simple stretching exercises.

'Ready Number Ten, here it comes.'

Whoosh – the ball was released. I watched it climb to an enormous height in a great curving arc. I ran forward to take the catch, squinting at the sky, my eyes filling with tears from the blinding glare of the sun. What made it even more difficult was my linebacker's helmet, which was totally unsuitable, and I cursed the protective grille. Then the ball began its descent. I had lost sight of it completely by now and just prayed it would somehow land in my waiting arms. It fell from the sky (so I'm told) like a stone and dropped directly on top of my helmet. I was knocked over, and the ball, so I'm reliably informed, bounced some forty yards into the arms of a spectator.

'Nice trick, Number Ten,' said one of the watching coaches.

'Good header, Max,' said our sound recordist.

Our film cameraman, a certain Gerry Hall, was helpless with laughter and collapsed to the ground. Mercifully for me, because of this, the film footage was never shown on television.

It was explained to me later that it was common practice to look away from the bright sun for *some* of the duration of the ball's flight, hazard a guess as to the ball's direction and then look up again to take the catch.

I attempted a further ten of these 'launches' and was successful with only two. When I finally caught one cleanly after several attempts the big watching crowd gave me a resounding cheer and I punched the air as if I'd sunk a forty-foot putt to win the British Open.

However, one dour, humourless spectator and obviously avid Cowboy fan walked over to me. He had no way of knowing who I was or what we were doing. He assumed quite naturally that I was a serious contender for the vacant Dallas Cowboys punt receiver position. He came up to me and said, 'You're shit man!!!'

I tried various other positions that week and fared a little better as a 'punter' and as a 'kicker'. I found the ball was a little smaller than a conventional rugby ball and much harder. It was therefore much more difficult to kick. However, I did manage to get a 'hang time' of 5.001 seconds (the length of time the ball was in the air). Anything less than five seconds for the other rookie kickers would result in them being sent home.

The Dallas Cowboys' kicker was Raphael Septien, and I very rarely saw him miss a kick, even in practice. It was he who introduced me to the 'time capsule', a long cylindrical container filled with a heavy saline solution. Players who had had insufficient rest or sleep would lie floating horizontally in the container. The container door would be closed and the player left in an inky blackness and complete and utter silence. (Apparently it was impossible to sink.) It was claimed that an hour of sleep in this revolutionary way was equal to eight or ten hours' normal sleep.

I hesitantly crawled in and lay there for what seemed hours but, perhaps because of a long-time fear of drowning, I emerged an hour later completely covered in white crystals and not having slept a wink.

After several weeks of working out – being hurt and knocked about, notably whilst training as a 'nose tackle' with the defence – I trudged wearily back to the changing-rooms aching all over.

I found myself in the showers with one of the linebackers. Stripped off he was the biggest man I had ever seen.

He was a magnificent black man who towered above me. As he stood there in his nakedness, I couldn't help but look . . . to see if he was uniformly proportioned and if all the old wives' tales were true . . .

I stood there in a mixture of awe, envy and admiration. Finally I plucked up enough courage to ask him. The conversation went something like this:

'Has it always been like that?'

'No, I had to work on it.'

'What did you do?'

'All you need is a short piece of string and a brick.'

I went away with great reservations about trying it.

However, three weeks later he rang me up to ask how things had gone.

'How' ya doing, boy?'

'I'm all right,' I stammered.

'Did you do what I said?'

'Yes.'

'Did it work, boy?'

'Well, sort of . . .'

'What do you mean – sort of?'

'Well,' I said, 'It's gone black . . .'

By this time it had been explained to the producer of the film that it would not be possible for me to take any active part in any real game, practice or otherwise.

However one chance happening changed all that.

I had spent a bruising and frustrating morning with the linebackers, who were working out with the tackling bag. This was a great heavy bag (similar to the ones used by boxers) with which these huge men, many of them weighing over twenty stone, practised tackling. They would charge rhino-like at the bag, lower their shoulder and drive it back against a huge coiled spring until it locked on to a ratchet on the end of a long shaft.

Failing to drive the bag fully to the end of this very powerful spring resulted in the spring recoiling the player back.

Even for these big men it required a great deal of effort, but for me, weighing as I did then around one hundred and fifty pounds, it was almost impossible.

I watched them run at the bag from around five yards, drop their shoulders and drive it jolting back. To have any chance I had to run at it from a good twenty yards, gathering momentum like a runaway goods van before hurling myself at this bag, much to the delight of the rest of the squad.

I very nearly managed to power it back fully, but then

found myself thrown back, and ridiculed by the other players and taunted with shouts of 'Go practise with a bean bag, Max!'

This of course was followed with howls of laughter.

Later that night I returned alone to the deserted training area, which was well away from the main campus where the other players were resting.

I practised hitting the bag back time and time again until I managed to drive it all the way back against the spring.

Coach Landry, who, unknown to me and just by chance, had been walking that way, heard the 'jolts' of the steel apparatus and came over to see me.

He looked at me and, with almost a trace of a smile, said, 'You watch you don't bust that bag, Number Ten.'

From that one chance moment, I had gained his respect and he allowed us every facility and help, even suggesting I might make it to the first pre-season friendly at Texas Stadium back in Dallas.

He suggested I should try out as a running back (which is the equivalent of a centre in rugby).

'All you gotta do is run hard, run low and watch out for the big guys.'

The running back coach taught me a few plays and eventually we settled on one, a simple play called 'Blue Toss 39 Right'.

This was my invitation into a proper game, albeit in training.

The centre would snap it back to the quarterback, who would throw a lateral pass to me, by which time a 'crack' should have appeared in the opposition's defence (created for me by the blockers). I was then to accelerate through for a possible touch-down . . . !!!

I asked the coach how much of a gap would there be and was told: 'All you need, Max, is *eight inches of daylight.*'

We took up our offensive line-up position, did the famous Dallas Cowboy Shuffle, and then the quarterback called the play Blue Toss 39 Right – Hut! Hut!

The ball was snapped back, the quarterback took it and

threw a lovely spiralling pass to me. Mercifully I took it cleanly and ran to the right, looking for the promised 'crack' in the opposition's defence.

Admittedly I did see it, albeit briefly, and then it 'healed' up again.

I was now looking for any way through, and driven only by instinct. I sidestepped this twenty stone 'defensive end' who was bearing down on me and then sheer fright slanted me, Barry John style, past another, only to be flattened from behind.

I had gained *two whole yards* – and dislocated three fingers.

The coach called me over and said, 'Number Ten, what you did there, you can't teach. That ain't in any coaching manual. You cut back against the grain and caused a lot of people to miss. Do you know that?'

I knew he wasn't serious but I still felt elated, I had gained *two whole yards* and I showed off my dislocated fingers like a child with a cut knee. I didn't dare complain, however, for I had been told: 'You have to learn to play with pain.'

'What happened to the eight inches of daylight?' I asked.

'It was there, Number Ten – it was there! But they saw you's a coming, and switched it off.'

However, I had impressed enough for them to persevere with this new 'running back' (even if it was just for the sake of the film). I went to sleep that night with a deep feeling of satisfaction that they had at last found a place for me.

We were now in the last few days of training camp and the rookies had been reduced to about five (and me). Training became even harder and more involved, with each session being videoed to be re-run and analysed later that night. I particularly hated the ten gruelling hundred-yard sprints in full gear that ended each sesion. However, I had now lost a stone and a half and was considerably stronger and fitter.

So God Could Watch the Cowboys Play

At the end of the week I was sad to leave the campus where I had experienced so much over the weeks. We headed back to Dallas to prepare for the first pre-season game against the Green Bay Packers.

I was astounded to learn that all the tickets for this game and all the other Dallas Cowboy games for the rest of the season were already sold out. I began to feel very nervous at the thought of playing in front of 75,000 people (none of whom had ever heard of me . . . !)

The plan was that if the Cowboys were leading by a sufficient margin with minutes to go, I was to run the last few plays including the play I had made my own – 'Blue Toss 39 Right on Two'.

Texas Stadium was quite magnificent, with everyone seated. The playing surface was synthetic and the facilities quite superb. The stadium was not completely covered, which prompted me to write a song about 'America's team' – the chorus of which went:

> They left a hole in the roof they say
> *So God could watch the 'Cowboys' play.*
> He's up there oh! – yes siree.
> I can't see him,
> But he'll see me,
> Cos they left a hole . . .

I hardly slept the night before the game, and when I did I dreamt only of making seventy-five-yard touch-downs. The morning came eventually. I couldn't wait to get to the ground.

I felt nervous as I changed into my uniform. I asked one

of the linebackers to adjust the straps on my helmet, and he locked it on tightly. I thanked him and explained that it had never fitted properly and the last thing I wanted was to have my helmet moving about. Especially if I was hit hard about the head.

Before the game, coach Landry gave us a brief talk. No one moved, and no one said a word. He spoke quietly in a voice that penetrated everything and everybody.

'OK, we are all prepared, but before I send you out there, I'm going to give you all a minute with your maker . . .'

Every member of the team knelt.

Seeing all these big men with huge shoulder pads, kneeling quietly in prayer, touched me deeply and seemed somehow unreal. Then in all that stillness coach Landry spoke to me, his voice reverberating around the room.

'Number Ten, take your helmet off!'

I mumbled an apology and fumbled with the tightly drawn straps. I felt so embarrassed as the whole team, God, and coach Landry waited for me to remove my helmet.

We eventually took the field, each member of the 'offence' was introduced individually to the huge adoring popcorned crowd. The commentator's voice boomed out over the P.A. system.

'Wearing Number 86 from Michigan State – Butch Johnston.'

The crowd roared their approval, and the lines of cheerleaders high-kicked their appreciation, balloons burst and the band played.

'Wearing Number 33 – Tony Dorsett.'

The crowd erupted once more.

Then it came to my turn.

'Wearing Number Ten, from Trefforest School of Mines – Wales – Running Back – Max Boyce.'

I ran on, waving to the crowd, hoping I wouldn't trip over, in my unashamed excitement.

The crowd roared, and then turned to each other and asked, 'Who the f . . . . that?'

I was made very welcome by the rest of the 'offence' and did the customary 'high five' hand-slapping routine. I then retired to the bench on the sidelines and waited my call . . . and waited and waited.

I watched the twists and turns of the Cowboys' fortunes and saw them unaccountably fall behind in a game they had been expected to win easily. I sat there for over three hours, in a confused state of expectancy, nervous apprehension and hope, trying to appear unconcerned.

When the final whistle blew, the Cowboys having lost narrowly, I was totally exhausted, and bitterly disappointed. The crowd hadn't seen my 'Blue Toss 39'.

I subsequently wrote this song to accompany the sad ending to the film:

Hey! Mr Landry, I'm here, I'm Number Ten.
I'm just sitting waiting, you just tell me when,
I'll give them all a shock when they see me run amock.
There's a new kid on the block – Mr Landry.

Hey! Mr Landry, I'm still waiting for your call.
Can it be that you don't mean to use me after all?
It looks and seems to me, it's there for all to see,
You have no faith in me – Mr Landry.

Hey! Mr Landry, I'll be more than just dismayed
What'll I tell my friends when they ask me how I played?
I'm not the best that's been, but I'm more than kinda keen,
I'm looking pretty mean – Mr Landry.

Hey! Mr Landry, I've been sitting here awhile.
I've been sitting hoping, trying hard to smile.
But you never gave me a chance,
Not so much as a second glance.
You never gave me a chance – Mr Landry.

My first visit down under in 1978 was a mixture of great concert success and desperate frustration. I was touring at the same time as the Welsh Rugby Team, and the promoters of my tour, surprisingly, were the Australian Rugby Union. What they lacked in professional expertise, they made up for in enthusiasm, with the result that I found myself thrust on every conceivable television programme to promote the concerts, regardless of their suitability.

At one point I found myself on a gardening programme because they'd been told I had a nine-foot leek!

I tried to make it entertaining by saying that I also grew the biggest onions in South Wales and that just before I came to Australia my mother had been peeling one in Cardiff and there were people crying in Swansea . . .

But undoubtedly the most unfortunate experience, apart from being asked 'What's a Pontypool?', was on a programme for five to nine-year-olds called *Fat Cat and Friends*, which went out live at seven in the morning.

After having got to the studio at a ridiculous hour on what

47

was only my second day in Australia, I sat somewhat jet-lagged and weary in my dressing-room, listening to our press agent.

'I want you to jump out of the set, Max. All Australia watch Fat Cat with their kids. This is a big chance for us to sell a lot of tickets in Wollongong, which is, as you know Max, dragging its feet.'

I nodded, trying to show some enthusiasm, and explained I was very concerned to meet Fat Cat to ascertain some common ground and maybe to agree on some questions he could feed me, so as to avoid any more like 'What's a Pontypool?' and 'What's that railway station with the long name?'

It transpired, when I finally met the producer, that this was going to be much more difficult than I'd imagined.

'Fat Cat,' he explained, 'doesn't meet anyone once he's in costume. Once he's changed he actually believes he's a cat . . . and lives the part in every way. I'm sorry.'

I just stared at the producer in disbelief but thought that if I got to meet Fat Cat I could probably reason with him.

Fat Cat turned out to be a huge brown furry thing which resembled a bear more than a cat, a good seven feet tall, with big protruding eyes and long whiskers. I approached him with some trepidation and held out my hand.

'Hello, I'm Max Boyce. I'm a guest on today's programme, and as I only arrived here from London yesterday and have never seen the programme I wondered if we could have a chat over a cup of coffee before we actually record?'

'Purr! Purr!' went Fat Cat and dabbed at me playfully with a huge brown paw. 'Purr! Purr!'

I was completely taken aback. (Needless to say the band were helpless with laughter.) Despite feeling rather embarrassed I carried on: 'Listen, Fat Cat, I admire your professionalism and your theatricality, but I know you're not a cat and, deep down, you *must* know you're not a cat, so can we please have a little talk?'

There was an awkward silence and then he actually went for me, spitting and attempting to scratch me, before

bounding off across the studio.

'You've upset him now,' said the floor manager and ran off after him (no doubt with a saucer of milk).

The producer came over again. 'I did tell you, Mr Boyce. However, I do sympathise with you. Listen, why don't you go and see Percy, who co-presents the programme? He's in dressing-room four. He should be of some help to you.'

Much relieved, I set off to look for Percy.

I knocked on the dressing-room door.

'Yes, c'mon in,' said a friendly enough voice.

I entered, only to be faced with . . . a nine-foot penguin.

I stumbled from one interview to the next and from one journalist to another, but I was assured by our publicist, 'It's beginning to take effect. Since yesterday, we've sold another two in Wollongong.' The concerts did however 'pick up' eventually, with the result that we had to move to bigger venues in some of the cities.

Eventually the time came for our first concert in Australia in the lovely city of Perth. After all the frustration I couldn't wait to get on stage, and at last I was what could only be described as unleashed from my dressing-room.

The overwhelming reception we received that night confirmed there was no need to adjust my material to include red-back spiders and Ayers Rock.

It was in Perth I first met a remarkable lady from Llanelli who came to every concert and to every game that Wales played in Australia.

On the eve of the last Test in Sydney she turned up at the theatre with a gift of two warm Welsh faggots. When I thanked her, she explained that she had made thirty more for the Welsh team and asked where they were staying. I told her, and on the morning of the game she went round to their hotel in Kings Cross at half past eight with thirty warm Welsh faggots. Clive Rowlands, the team manager, accepted the gift and assured her that the 'boys' would have them for breakfast.

As events turned out, Wales lost that ill-tempered Test, and at the sour, unhappy after-match function the first person I met was this woman, her eyes all swollen red, tears streaming down her face.

'Oh, Max!' she said. 'Did you see the game?'

I answered that I had, and told her not to upset herself so. 'Oh, Max!' she said. 'Do you think it was the faggots?'

I was telling the story again on a television programme the following Monday, and even before the punchline, the studio audience were falling about laughing.

What I didn't know then was that the word 'faggot' had a totally different meaning in Australia and the audience had interpreted that the reason Wales lost was that before the game this woman from Llanelli had taken round to the Welsh team's hotel *thirty warm Welsh homosexuals*!

A week later I was invited to appear on a programme called the *Peter Couchman Show*, an afternoon magazine programme. I was to be one of several celebrity guests, including a Greek restaurateur (as it was Greek Week in Melbourne).

I was interviewed, sang a song, and then the host turned to the restaurateur and invited him to explain the dish he was about to prepare in the studio.

In broken English he explained, 'Today, for you, I make *Calamari Athenia.*' He then proceeded to cook some squid in a large thermostatically controlled frying-pan. With suitable theatricality he added certain herbs and wine and the occasional tall story.

Because the dish was taking longer than had been anticipated, Peter Couchman decided to take a brief commercial break. During the break the restaurateur, a certain Spiros Andreos, became rather agitated and explained that for some reason the frying-pan was not reaching the required temperature. But he asked whether I would taste his dish anyway, pretending it was excellent fare, and adding that I would be welcome at his restaurant together with my family and friends.

Realising his embarrassment, I thanked him for his kind offer and explained there was no need, I would be only too glad to help him out of his difficulty.

'Welcome back,' announced Peter Couchman at that moment. 'You're just in time to hear Max Boyce's appraisal of the culinary art of Mr Andreos and his *Calamari Athenia* here, live on the *Peter Couchman Show.*'

I was passed this portion of limp squid on a long fork.

Now, I have found squid a little rubbery at the best of times, but this uncooked *Calamari Athenia* was like eating something out of a bicycle repair kit. I rolled it round in my mouth and made all the suitable noises – 'Umm! Ah!' then,

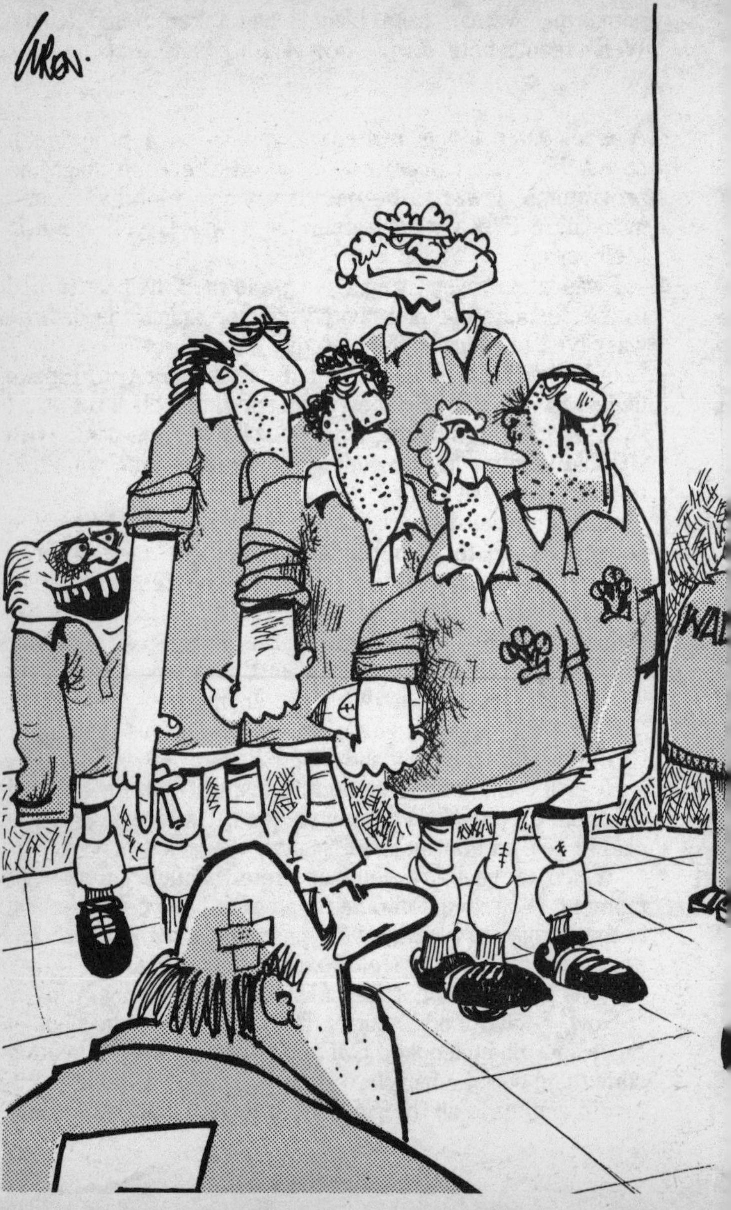
Gren.

through a half-opened mouth, declared that it was truly superb.

'There,' said the host. 'You have it. The totally unbiased opinion of a European's view of a classic Greek dish prepared by our good friend Spiros Andreos.' He then proceeded to wind up the programme. 'Well, that's all we have for you today. My thanks to . . .'

I could see from the monitor facing me that I was no longer in shot, so I hastily and thankfully took from my mouth this foul-tasting, half-cooked, slimy rubber ball and held it in my hand.

The show's presenter went on, 'My thanks also to my producer, our sponsors and, last but not least, our special guest and guinea pig, Mr Max Boyce. You've been a sport, Max. I'd like to shake your hand . . .'

I remember sitting in the lounge at Perth Airport in Western Australia about to be interviewed by Channel Seven Television about the prospects for the Welsh Rugby Team's imminent tour there, when an elderly Welsh supporter leaned into the conversation, thrust a can of Felinfoel Double Dragon into my hand and said in Welsh:

'Tell 'em, Max. There's no need of Radox in Bangkok.' He had just arrived on a supporter tour from Britain and en route had stopped over for three nights in Bangkok, where some of the party had visited one of Thailand's infamous bath-houses.

'I didn't think it would be any use me going really, Max,' he went on. 'See, the old seam's worked out and I thought to myself, what could these young girls do with "old workings"? – But I was surprised . . . do you know what they did?'

We all ashamedly leaned forward – a Sunday school distance – trying not to look interested, and then I asked, as casually as I could, 'What did they do?'

He drew us closer and said, 'They cut my bloody toenails!

54

What I really needed, Max, was a younger man and some jump leads!'

We all roared with laughter and I couldn't help wondering, for weeks afterwards, whether the Thailand Tourist Board would ever make use of that marvellous phrase: 'There's no need of Radox in Bangkok!'

You Won't Remember Me, But...

*I*t has always amused and pleased me that so many Welsh people, when they move away from the principality, suddenly become very conscious of their Welshness. This has become even more evident to me during overseas tours. At the end of every concert there would inevitably be a very nice Welsh lady waiting for me. She would be carrying a biscuit tin covered loosely with a blue check tablecloth and behind her at a Sunday school distance would be her husband wearing a sheepish grin, red socks and a faded Triple Crown tie. The kindly Welsh lady would approach me, tears in her smiling eyes, almost unable to speak with emotion, and thrust the tin into my hands.

'I made them specially for you . . .'
'Welshcakes!!'

Welsh Cakes (Pics ar y Maen)   *(Makes about 20)*

8 oz plain flour	½ teaspoon baking powder
2 oz butter or margarine	¼ teaspoon mixed spice
2 oz lard	1 egg
3 oz sugar	pinch of salt
2 oz currants	milk to mix

Sift flour, baking powder, salt and spice together, rub in mixed fats (use all butter for traditional taste). Add sugar and currants, bind with beaten egg to a stiff paste, similar to shortcrust pastry. Roll out to about ¼ inch thick, and cut into 2½ inch rounds. Bake on a greased bakestone for about 3 mins each side until golden brown. Sprinkle with sugar and eat hot or cold.

I doubt if there is anyone, apart from the Morriston Orpheus Male Choir, who has eaten more welshcakes than me. I am convinced that these kindly people think I can't survive more than a couple of hours without having a 'fix'. The worst thing is they watch me eating them as if they are waiting for a physical change to take place. I, in turn, smile through the sugary crumbs and sigh, my system no longer racked by withdrawal symptoms.

I have secretly worried about being 'hooked' on welsh-cakes and in time, no doubt, when I am no longer undertaking overseas tours, I will sorely miss them. I probably will end up searching for some 'pusher' in the twilight areas of cities like Sydney and Toronto who peddles inferior imported welshcakes (made in Taiwan) and long to see a check tablecloth again. I will in all probability join 'Welshcakes Anonymous' and be urged to talk to others about my problem. No doubt the first thing I will be asked to do is to stand in front of a meeting and admit to it.

'I am a welshcakaholic.'

No doubt there will be the inevitable death from such addiction and the story carried in the unfortunate person's local paper back home in Wales:

'. . . formerly of 37 Cemetery Road, Tonypandy, was found dead in his apartment at Woolomoloo, Australia, in the early hours of yesterday morning. He had drunk a bottle of whiskey and eaten thirty-four welshcakes. He left a son and . . . two welshcakes.'

I have sometimes wondered whether Scottish and Irish entertainers have similar experiences. Does Billy Connolly get besieged with haggis, and Dave Allen with great bowls of steaming Irish broth?

It is also quite astonishing how distances and places become rather flexible and blurred to people who have lived away from home for some time. I remember once in Hong Kong waiting to take the stage for the second half of our concert and my road manager coming up to me and saying:

'Max, there's a bloke outside the stage door who says he lived in the next village to you for twenty years and he'd love to meet you. I told him you don't like seeing anybody before you go on, but he says he can't wait till the end of the show as the last train to Shang Ling goes at ten.'

'Oh!' I said. 'Bring him in.'

We shook hands and I expected him to say he was from Cwmgwrach or Rhigos, the villages close to where I live in Glynneath, West Glamorgan.

'Where are you from, then?' I asked.

'Swindon,' he replied.

Despite countless gifts of welshcakes, there has only been one occasion when I have been brought that other traditional Welsh delicacy, laverbread and cockles.

They were given to me by a lovely lady from the Gower who we met in Toronto, Canada. She told me the wonderful story of how one day 'Old Annie', a famous old cockle

woman from Penclawdd (a little village near Swansea), was gathering cockles in the wet silt of the Burry Estuary.

Old Annie hitched up her flounced skirts and petticoats and stooped to gather cockles in the time-honoured tradition before loading them by the sackful on to a cart to be taken by donkey across the wet sands for sale in Swansea market.

One day apparently the donkey broke free of the cart and showed what could be only described as 'a passing interest in old Annie'.

Annie, without turning around, said, 'I don't know who you are or where you are from, but I'm here every Monday, Wednesday and Friday.'

It has always amazed me to find people waiting to welcome us on arrival at airports all over the world. I have never been able to work out how they came to know our arrival times but unfailingly they would be there, gathered in the airport terminal, some dressed in Welsh costume, others waving flags and banners. There were even some 'Max Boyce' lookalikes – women with curly black wigs wearing red and white scarves and brandishing leeks and daffodils of all shapes and sizes.

I told them the true story of a pretty young girl from Derbyshire who had done a similar thing. She and her mother had entered a carnival in which there was a fancy dress competition. Apparently there were two categories, one for the best individual and the other for the best 'pair' or 'couple'. She went on to say how she had entered the competition dressed as 'Max Boyce' with the trailing red and white scarf, bobble hat and rosette and that her elderly mother had gone dressed as my 'leek'.

She said there had been hilarious moments 'building' the 'leek', partly because her mother's glasses kept steaming up inside it and she couldn't see where she was going. She kept bumping into people and knocking things over. Because of this problem they decided to enter for the best pair category so that her mother could be led by the hand. The day of the carnival arrived and there were many entries for the best pair including Batman and Robin, Rod Hull and Emu and the Lone Ranger and Tonto.

I told her I was flattered she and her mother had gone to so much trouble and enquired if they had been placed in the competition.

'Oh,' she said. 'We didn't come anywhere. The judge had never heard of you . . . but we weren't too disappointed . . . the leek came second in the individual section.'

A Weekend in Singapore

*M*y first visit to Singapore was almost a disaster. Much against my better judgement, I agreed to perform in cabaret for two nights in a large hotel, with a meal being included in the price of the ticket.

Our promoter, the unflappable William Thomson, had 'sold' the concerts to the hotel with the guarantee I would sell out *two* nights in Singapore. The owner had agreed to the deal, knowing the profit he could make on food and beverages.

I stressed to Bill that I doubted the wisdom of taking on two nights, but he was unrelenting. 'It'll be all right,' Bill said. 'Trust me!'

When we arrived in Singapore, we were all detained by immigration officials who demanded that the band have their hair cut to an acceptable length – worse was to follow.

After booking into the hotel, we learnt that the first night's concert was almost sold out, but only twelve tickets had been sold for the second.

Despite heated discussions with the manager, he refused to consider a cancellation, insisting he'd prepared for two nights. He argued quite fairly that we should be responsible for any surplus food. This meant us having to account for 478 soups, chicken dinners and sherry trifles.

Bill immediately impressed on the band the need to fast as some hearty eating would be called for.

The first night was an unqualified success, and I ended by telling the audience of our problem concerning the meals and appealed to them, suggesting that *if* they had enjoyed the evening, they should *tell a friend* and explain there were still '*a few tickets left for tomorrow night . . .*'

The audience must have felt genuinely sorry for us, for many of them attended the concert again on the second night and brought crowds of their friends. It turned out to be an unforgettable night, with the band taking sips of soup and spoonfuls of trifle between songs.

It even turned out that we had more in the audience for the second concert than the first.

'What did I tell you?' said Bill.

'We could have done *three* nights. . .'

Rodeo

*F*ollowing the success of the American football film, Opix Films wanted to find another suitable adventure for me along the same lines. We had discussed various ideas and, while we were reliving the Dallas Cowboy experience one night, someone came up with 'rodeo'.

I laughed and explained at once I had always had a fear of horses ever since I went pony trekking down the Gower

coast and flirted with a Ford Cortina on the B road to Oxwich. A friend of mine who was an accomplished horseman had persuaded me to come riding with him. He explained it was only a little more than pony trekking. He lent me all the correct clothing – jodhpurs, helmet, boots, etc. – and we arrived at this farm in the Gower near Swansea.

As the horses were being matched up to the prospective riders, my fears subsided. The horses were old and ponderous, with names like Daisy and Bluebell. I faked disappointment. Unfortunately the instructor registered this and said, 'It's all right, follow me.'

He took me to this corral where some other horses were kept. He had assumed, because of my attitude on seeing the older horses and my borrowed gear, that I too was an accomplished rider. He led this horse out and I feebly asked the instructor its name, expecting a Pip or another Bluebell.

'Geronimo,' he replied.

I shuddered.

'He can be a bit of a handful,' the instructor went on. 'Keep him on a tight rein.'

My friend helped me to mount up and adjusted the stirrups. I plodded off with the others down the path that led from the farm. It was all very pleasant and enjoyable until we came to where we had to cross the main road. All the other horses pulled up and began chewing and pulling at the long grass, respectful of the holiday traffic. Geronimo, however, went stubbornly on despite my frantic attempts to hold him back. His ears pricked up and we were away. I hung on grimly as we narrowly missed a car pulling a long caravan. The driver understandably shook his fist and frantically blew the car's horn, which only served to drive the horse even wilder. He galloped away down the steep woodland that led through the gorse and the bramble to Oxwich Bay, picking his way through a thicket of silver birch, seemingly bent on decapitating his rider on the branches of every low-hanging tree.

We arrived somehow at Oxwich Bay, where Geronimo thankfully slowed down and pulled up on the wet sand. I had been terrified, but somehow I had managed to stay on. The instructor arrived with the others some twenty minutes later, rode over to me and said, 'Take it easy on the way back – *some of these people haven't ridden before . . .*'

I swore there and then that I would never have anything to do with horses ever again.

The producer heard me out, but was not convinced. He continued to try to persuade me.

'It'll be the best thing you've ever tried,' he argued.

However, I still wasn't at all happy with the thought of riding wild horses, and asked for some time to think it over.

The very next morning the producer rang excitedly and said, 'We've managed to raise the money to film rodeo in Colorado, and the Professional Rodeo Cowboys' Association have agreed to take you on. We fly out a week tomorrow. It's to be a co-production with the BBC. What do you think?'

He admitted that a week was no time to prepare and that it was asking an awful lot. It could presumably also be very dangerous. Would I attempt it? Despite my genuine fears, I thrilled at the enormous challenge and agreed.

The BBC in Wales made immediate arrangements for me to have some lessons at a riding school near Caerphilly, a place called Graig Fawr Farm. The people that owned and ran the stables, a Mr and Mrs Dennis Jones and their sons, were warm friendly people and tried to put me at ease. Mr Jones's son Andrew was to be my instructor. He stressed it normally took a year to learn to ride properly but he would do what he could in the few days that we had. He brought me a horse. I prayed it wouldn't be called Geronimo.

The time I spent with the Dallas Cowboys at their training camp at Thousand Oaks in California was an exhausting and gruelling one. The bruises eventually faded but the friendships lasted, notably those with Billy Joe Dupree (Number 89) and Ed 'Too Tall' Jones (Number 72) – a member of the Cowboys' legendary 'Doomsday Defence'.

My first bull ride lasted 1.6 seconds – of which I remember
nothing but the violent surging of the animal. The cowboys
didn't seem too concerned for my safety riding bulls, but were
surprisingly anxious during the time I spent steer wrestling
(below). This involved riding flat-out on a quarter-horse,
hurling yourself at a moving 300-pound horned steer and
wrestling it to the ground. On reflection, I was lucky to escape
unhurt.

Following the rodeo circuit was one of the most exhilarating experiences of my life, and the rodeo cowboys were some of the friendliest, most genuine people I've ever met. I shared the fortunes of a bull rider 'going down the road', and for a time I took on the guise of an old bull rider turned mountain man ('Folks just call me "Colorado" '). Miraculously, the trout I caught in the clear mountain streams were already filleted ...

My training as a rodeo cowboy included learning the skills of the 'barrel men', who worked in tandem with the bull-fighting clowns to lure the bull away from a fallen rider. The action sequence (left) shows 'Barrel-man Boyce' in the hermit-crab position in the Cheyenne Frontier Days Rodeo – where the smile was just painted on me.

The bull-fighting clowns had my utmost admiration for their courage and skill. The older rodeo clowns dressed in the traditional circus manner and entertained the crowds in the time-honoured way. They were there to add a touch of colour and laughter to the rodeo circuit, but there was also real danger involved in working so close to wild bulls.

My journey to Nepal to take part in the World Elephant Polo Championship was varied, to say the least. It proceeded via a series of hollowed-out boats, rope bridges and the inevitable elephant. The people we met were friendly and welcoming. I found myself wondering at their different faith and culture, and about the one-eyed yellow idol to the north of Katmandu . . .

The World Elephant Polo Championship was perhaps the most bizarre sporting event I have ever witnessed – let alone participated in. It was held near the Tiger Tops jungle lodge in the Chitwan National Park. I played 'up-front' for the Cartier team – my fellow team members being Billy Connolly, Ringo Starr and his wife Barbara Bach. It was like playing golf with a fishing rod, sitting astride a double-decker bus with a puncture ...

Travelling to the strange and distant lands of the Middle East called for a great deal of tolerance and adaptability on the part of the road-crew and the band. At a typical rehearsal sound check outdoors in Bahrain (above), my faithful musician John Luce was somewhat overcome by the desert heat.

Below (right) is a portrait of my 'genuine' leek in concert in Dubai, and (left) one of a fancy-dress imposter (see page 60).

What followed proved to be one of the most embarrassing moments of my life. I had purposely worn jeans that day and found they were much too tight to enable me to mount the horse properly. Eventually we were forced to make use of a milk crate to enable me to mount my steed. As fate had it, some students from University College Cardiff were at the farm at the same time on a riding course. They recognised me 'astride my crate' and came over. They had been watching with great amusement as I tried to mount this great big horse, and asked what I was doing there. I filled with embarrassment as I stepped down from my crate and explained: *'I'm going to be a rodeo cowboy in Cheyenne.'*

A few looked at me disbelievingly, while others sniggered. One laughed and asked whether I was taking my crate as hand luggage.

Apart from that incident my first lesson was uneventful, and I agreed to return the next day and every day until I flew out to America. My instructor pushed me as hard as he could in the days that followed and, despite a few hard falls, I think he was pleased with my progress. I had now begun to enjoy riding and was secretly thrilled at the challenge. Deep down, however, there was a strange foreboding, for I knew in my heart that riding a 'coop' horse on a Caerphilly mountain was hardly preparation for Cheyenne.

Colorado Springs

My friends at the farm wished me well, and a week later I arrived in Colorado Springs together with the film crew. The next day we drove out to the ranch where I would be staying. It was owned by a Mr Harry Volt, one of the biggest stock contractors in America, who supplied bulls, horses and steers for all the big rodeos. He was a gruff but friendly man and instantly admonished me for my clothing, and particularly my 'fancy shoes'. Apparently the ranch, 'Rattlesnake Butte', was infested with rattlesnakes and cowboy boots were essential. I casually asked what would happen if you were bitten.

Harry Volt called out to the cowboys who worked for him to come over. They were called Mad Dog, Preacher Paul, Chuck and Brad.

'Boys, this is Max Boyce. He's a movie star from over there in England and he's gonna be making a movie here.'

I didn't dare correct him and felt so out of place in my Jaeger blazer and fawn trousers (which the director had insisted I should wear) and I knew how ridiculous I must have looked to these ranch hands.

'I want you boys to show him round and, Preacher Paul, get him some proper clothes. He looks like he's selling ice cream . . .'

Preacher Paul, a big, warm, friendly man who had been converted to Christianity during his time as a marine with the American navy in Vietnam, was to teach me to ride and help me live the life of a cowboy.

I explained that I had very little experience and, because of this, had been advised to wear ladies tights under my jeans to prevent my legs chafing on long rides.

He said, 'Tights? You mean pantihose?'

'Yes,' I stammered. 'I think so.'

He thought for a while and then said, 'Yeah, we had a guy out here before from England who did that. We fed him with beans, he passed gas and blew his boots off . . . Besides, Max, I wouldn't like the other cowboys in the bunk-house to catch you wearing pantihose. They're mean men. They ain't seen a woman in a long while, and what with your long eyelashes and them there pantihose, I wouldn't like to be responsible.'

I laughed and warmed to the big man.

The other cowboys, especially Brad, were much quieter and hardly spoke at all. I, meanwhile, babbled away in my nervousness, anxious to make an impression, and made small talk which I invariably regretted the minute I'd started speaking. In my nervousness I tended to speak quickly and I doubted sometimes whether they could understand me.

One night, after listening to me a while, Mad Dog said, 'That sure is a strange accent, Max. You sound just like a Cherokee Indian.'

I soon found that riding Western style was completely different to riding in an English saddle, and therefore negated much of what I had learnt at Graig Fawr. I persevered, however, and soon was heading for my first round-up on a horse they'd given me called Smoke Signal.

I had expected everyone to be involved, but it was to be just Brad and myself. We started out at first light, to protect the horses from the heat of the day, and rode some thirty miles to a box canyon to gather a herd of wild horses and a few bulls and steers.

Brad positioned me at one end of the canyon and then drove the herd through. Unfortunately, some three or four bulls broke away from the main bunch and Brad rode after them, shouting to me to take the main herd back the way we had come. I continued to drive them slowly back along the dusty trail, terrified to alter my position relative to the herd for fear of losing control of them. After about half a mile, I became less tense and started to relax, making suitable calls to the herd and slapping the side of my horse with my hat to drive a little calf along. I leant back in the saddle of my flea-bit grey, wishing those university students could see me now on my first 'gathering', driving a baying, bellowing herd of wild mustangs, steers and Brahma bulls down the dusty trail to Rattlesnake Butte. 'Clint Boyce, trail boss.'

Then Smoke Signal stepped in a prairie dog hole and stumbled, throwing me forward, clean over his head, and frightening the herd. They began to stampede and run in all directions, several wild-eyed horses hightailing it back the way we had just come. I was on the verge of panic, feeling both horrified and helpless, and it was several minutes before I remounted Smoke Signal. I attempted to get the herd back together, but it was hopeless. I succeeded with some, but the older, wilier animals had sensed my ineptitude and uncertainty and toyed with me like third-formers with a student teacher. A huge Brahma bull faced me defiantly, with one broken horn hanging uselessly by the side of his head. For one terrifying moment I was convinced he was going to charge, but then mercifully he turned and rejoined what was left of the herd.

I got back to the ranch eventually, soaked with perspiration and physically and mentally drained. I had lost five bulls, twenty-three horses and my hat. As I came back from the main corral I heard Brad returning. I rode over slowly and sheepishly explained what had happened. He looked at me for a long time and then said slowly:

'Max, there is one thing a cowboy should never lose and that's his hat. You see, Max, it keeps him from burning up, shields his eyes from the sun and holds water should he ever need it.'

I said, 'I'm sorry about the horses. I . . .'

He threw his head back and laughed. 'It's all right, boy, they're here.'

He had seen what had happened, ridden round in a circle and brought them all back, together with the strays he had rounded up.

As we rode back to the bunk-house, he tossed me my crumpled hat.

'Fancy a cold beer . . . ?'

Next morning the horses were branded and loaded into great wagons which would take them to the rodeo in Cheyenne.

> And I wondered next morning how wild horses feel
> To be hauled off to rodeos in cages of steel,
> Away from the mountains where once they ran free,
> For the sport and the pleasure of a cowboy like me.

My initiation into the competition side of rodeo began at the Professional Rodeo Cowboys' Association headquarters in Colorado Springs, where professional cowboys instructed me with the aid of a mechanical bull.

My first attempt to ride on this gyrating, jerking contraption nearly resulted in a dislocated neck and my right arm being ripped out of its socket.

The watching cowboys just laughed, shouting advice and slapping their sides.

'Keep your chin tucked in there, Max.'

'You got him Max, he's tiring . . .'

After several attempts I was convinced my right arm was several inches longer. (Would my suits ever fit me properly again?) However, I began to master the technique and wondered what resemblance it would have to a real bull.

Despite the fact that every bone in my body ached from my confrontation with the mechanical bull, I was to find that out the very next morning.

We were taken to a small ranch owned by a stock contractor called Swede. He was a kindly old man who had lived all his life with rodeo horses and bulls and supplied stock to the smaller rodeos. I liked him immediately. I sat enthralled as he told me hair-raising tales of the terrible injuries he had received. I was so taken with this utterly genuine old character that when he offered me some tobacco to chew I took some. I made the further mistake of saying (in foolish bravado), 'It's good . . .' and then swallowed some . . . I turned away as my eyes watered and was very nearly sick, but I wasn't going to show old Swede. He brought me some every day after that!

SO YOU WANT TO BE A BULLRIDER

'So you want to be a bullrider,
You want to be one too.
Well, I'm the only one who can teach you, son,
And I'll show you what to do.

'You just fill your mouth with marbles,'
That's what the old man said,
'Some orange, purple, blue and green,
Some yellow, white and red.'

So I did just as he'd told me,
Just as the old man said,
And I filled my mouth with marbles,
Some yellow, white and red.

'Then we'll enter every rodeo –
There's plenty here about –
And every time you see me ride
You spit a marble out.'

So we entered every rodeo
In towns I'd never seen –
Burlington and Henderson,
Cheyenne and Evergreen.

And I did just as he'd told me,
I rolled them marbles round,
And every time he rode a bull
A marble hit the ground.

Then came the day I had none left,
And I went and told him so.
He said, 'I guess you're ready then –
For the Pikes Peak Rodeo.

'Yeah! I guess you're ready now,
And your rope I'll gladly pull,
But you had to lose your marbles
'Fore I let you ride a bull.'

My first bull ride was one of the most exhilarating experiences of my life, and I shall never forget it as long as I live. I was very apprehensive, as indeed were all the television crew. The cowboys sensed this and assured me everything would be fine.

'Just cowboy it up, Max. You got enough want-to to make it.'

The bull they had selected for me to ride was called Smoky Joe, and I shuddered as I watched the cowboys drive him into one of the bucking chutes, his horns banging into the chute's timbered sides. I realised that now there was no going back, and worst of all, that *this* bull could not be set to buck slowly or for that matter be switched off at the mains.

A slow motion camera was located to one side of the arena while a second camera followed my fortunes in the chute area. The cowboys fitted some spurs to my boots and strapped a thick leather glove to my right hand.

'Okay now, Max, rub this resin in your glove and pull hard on this rope.'

The resin, through the friction of pulling, became tacky. This was done to help me grip the rope they would strap around the bull and prevent my hand from slipping.

The bull was still confined by the chute as I lowered myself quietly and gently on to his back. It bore no resemblance at all to sitting on the mechanical bull. The rolls of thick warm skin on the bull's back moved beneath me all the time and I nearly fell off in the chute.

The cowboys spoke quietly and earnestly and pulled the bucking rope tightly around the animal's back, trapping the back of my hand on to the bull. The loose end of the rope was then brought round for me to hold. My hand felt so tightly locked on that I was immediatley filled with another fear. Would my hand be ripped off when the bull threw me? I shuddered at the thought. The cowboys assured me that this 'rarely' happened.

'Rarely,' I repeated, half choking.

'Normally what happens, Max, is when a rider gets thrown the lead bell weights attached to the rope drag the rope clear and release your hand.'

'Normally . . . ?'

The cowboys were now talking me through the preliminaries.

'Scoot up on his back, Max – That's it – Now lean a little forward – Keep your chin tucked right in – Lock yourself in there – Good – You just nod when you're ready. Wait till his head is facing straight ahead or to the left before you nod, or he won't see the chute open.'

My free hand gripped the side of the gate as the bull moved impatiently around, pinning my left leg hard against the chute sides. I was aware of the sweat that was running down my back and that my breathing came in short stabs. I clenched my teeth and gripped the bull with all my strength.

'You ready, Max?'

I was about to nod when –

'Hold it! Hold it! It's no good, we'll have to stop.'

The sound recordist had picked up aircraft noise overhead.

'Hold it everybody,' said the producer. 'Cut.'

I dismounted and found my legs giving way. I cursed the fact that they had to stop filming. I had built myself up to a real 'high' of concentration, only to be told, 'Sorry, sweetie, we'll have to do it again . . .' It was cruel luck, and left me physically and mentally drained and in a terrible temper.

It was a while before I was ready to remount the bull and start the slow build-up all over again. I begged the producer, 'Don't stop me this time, whatever happens. I don't care if a hundred helicopters fly over. Keep filming.' He agreed.

Smoky Joe had become rather agitated by now at being confined in the chute for so long, and I was not at all welcome when I remounted. He stuck one horn into the side of the gate, splintering the timber, and clearly was not at all happy.

'Woah boy, stand back – Easy now.'

I waited until his head was in the right position . . . and nodded . . .

The gate was hauled open and the bull hurtled out of the chute. Although it was all happening so fast, I was instantly and acutely aware of the surging power of the animal beneath me as it bucked and twisted in an attempt to free itself of this appendage on its back. His very first buck had thrown me off balance and I clung on for dear life, all I had been taught forgotten.

He turned back to the right and bucked again, throwing me mercifully clear of his flying hooves.

'Stay down, Max!' the cowboys screamed. 'Stay down.'

The bull kicked high in the air, trying to rid itself of the kicking strap, and then turned back towards me. The cowboys moved between me and the bull and drove him back, snorting and kicking, to the relative freedom of his pen.

I had ridden my first bull.

The cowboys ran towards me, whooping with delight and shaking me warmly by the hand. I felt a tremendous feeling of elation and sense of achievement. I had stayed on for 1.6 seconds.

However short it had been, the sense of flirting on the cutting edge of danger had left me incredibly exhilarated,

and all I wanted at that moment was to ride again. Tommy laughed and understood the way I felt.

'I was kinda hoping you'd feel that way, Max . . . It gets you that way, don't it?'

I was more relaxed on my second ride and not nearly as nervous. I had experienced it once and some of my fears had subsided. I was still surprised myself, however, to find I was eager to ride wild bulls. Another bull was driven into the chute.

'When you're ready, Max.'

I nodded.

The gate was flung open a second time. This bull was skinnier and easier to ride, and I stayed on for 4.1 seconds.

In my foolishness, I forgot to 'stay down' after being thrown and the bull's rear legs clipped my forehead as I got up. I had in my mistaken bravado come very close to being seriously injured or possibly killed. I went cold at the thought and hoped it was a lesson learnt. I was also quietly pleased that I'd ridden two bulls, and now began to feel a deep sense of relief and also genuine closeness to the cowboys who had befriended and cared for me and talked me through my first bull rides.

'Fancy a cold beer?' asked Tommy.

We went to a place where they served 'Surf and Turf'. I was told to order a 'T' bone steak – to get my own back. . .

> Hey bull, I know you don't know me
> I'm just a boy amongst men
> I know you don't know me
> But if you don't throw me
> I'll never eat sirloin again. . .

That night I rang some dear friends back home and told them I'd ridden seven bulls and one for over two minutes . . .

76

The next day I was to try steer wrestling. This involved riding after a steer which had been released from a chute, throwing yourself from the horse, and wrestling the steer to the ground.

Seriously, for some unknown reason this held no fear for me, despite the fact that the bull riders were very apprehensive about me trying it because of the very real dangers involved. I agreed to practise on a plastic steer's head mounted on a bale of hay until I felt confident. I quite happily rode up to the bale of hay, threw myself at it with reckless abandon, grabbed the head's plastic horns and wrestled the steer to the ground. This produced gales of laughter from the watching cowboys, especially when I very nearly impaled myself on the steel spike attached to the plastic head.

I then attempted to wrestle a real steer and throw him to the ground. This was not easy and I struggled in vain with this poor creature, hoping I wasn't hurting him. Then along came the real thing.

The steer was driven into a little chute and I backed my horse alongside. When I was ready and in position, the steer was released and he shot forward (aided by a six-volt prod in his rear end). My horse charged after him until we drew alongside and I was looking down at the steer. It suddenly seemed a long way down and those horns I was supposed to grab hold of were real.

'Now, Max!' shouted the shoot man. 'Now! Jump!'

I leant out of my saddle until I was over the steer's back and then leapt. I touched one horn, albeit briefly, and then the steer stepped nimbly out of the path of my despairing lunge and I landed with a great thud in a cloud of dust. I was momentarily winded and felt a stabbing pain in my backside. I had landed directly on the steel battery case of the radio mike transmitter which was in my back pocket. Even to this day, I have a bruise which reads 'British Patent Pending No 4516/1'.

I attempted to bring down this animal several times, sometimes over-running the steer and being trampled on and other times missing him altogether. I was, after an hour, very sore, badly bruised, and desperately disappointed that I hadn't been able to wrestle the steer to the ground. I felt a little better about it later, when it was explained to me that it took months to be able to wrestle steers. I'd honestly thought it could be done in a single afternoon.

In the evening, I was taken to a masseur who attempted to get me into some sort of physical condition for the bare-back bronco riding that was scheduled for the next day. For the first time since I had arrived in Colorado I began to get a little disillusioned about wanting to become a cowboy, and asked the question:

> When will I get to ride off in the sunset,
> And hang around in smoky saloon bars?
> When will I get to draw and to tangle with the law,
> And sleep upon my saddle 'neath the stars?

Despite the massage, the tablets and the hot baths, I found when I awoke the next morning that every muscle in my body ached. I doubted very much whether I would be able to dress myself, let alone ride.

After a long discussion, the producer came up with an inspired suggestion: 'See how you feel when you get to the ranch.' Grimly I agreed.

The cowboys laughed when they saw me drag my aching body in, and suggested I'd be better off 'husk gathering in Arkansas' – which I took to be an insult.

'You have to learn to ride with pain, Max . . . What's the matter with you? Cowboy it up.'

At 10.30 I found myself back in the bucking chute, this time on a wild bare-back stallion called Steel. The procedure was the same as with the bulls: I was to nod when I was ready.

Despite my stiffness, I felt more at home on the horse, and a feeling of quiet resolve began to flow through me.

'Ready, Max?'

I nodded. The gate was hauled open once more.

The horse turned wild-eyed out of the chute and headed for the side of the corral with its high 'Kit Carson Fort' fences. I thought for one terrifying moment he was going to try and leap over, but he turned at the very last second, almost throwing me, and I hung perilously over the sharp pointed wall of logs that made up the fence. He continued galloping down the side of the arena and it was only sheer terror that kept me from being thrown.

I could hear the cowboys shouting and hollering, 'Hang on in there, Max! Stay with him!' And then I heard the most welcome sound I have ever heard. The sound of the buzzer that said I had stayed on for the required time. The horse continued to kick wildly, and then finally, as he turned at the end of the arena, sent me crashing into the wooden fence. Apart from a few scratches, I was unhurt and felt absolutely thrilled that I'd managed finally to complete an eight-second ride (albeit a rather ungainly one).

The cowboys rushed over to see if I was all right and shook me by the hand.

'Good ride. Good ride. You hung on in there.'

The old man who owned the little ranch rode over to me and said mockingly, 'Thought you said you could ride, boy. Seems to me the only thing you've ever ridden is a bar stool! We could tell what you was a-feeling when you heard that old hooter go . . . Shame you couldn't bottle it . . .'

After my week of intensive training, into which we'd crowded so much, it was decided that it would be impossible for me to compete in every rodeo event as was first hoped. I was to concentrate on becoming a bull rider – the one event that still filled me with apprehension.

Before that, however, I was to visit the most famous rodeo in America, Cheyenne Frontier Days, where I was to be taught some of the skills of a rodeo clown.

This Smile is
Just Painted on Me

The rodeo in the old frontier town of Cheyenne was held once a year and lasted for a week. It was here where the most famous cowboys in America pitted their wits, their skills and courage against the finest animals for the highest purses.

It was a week when the normally quiet suburban town relived memories of the wild frontier days of the old West. In the daytime, as well as the main rodeo events, there were 'wild horse' and 'chuck wagon' racing, while the nights that followed were full of a 'a-hooting and a-hollering' and the bars were full of fiddlers and banjo pickers playing country music.

Everyone was expected to dress the part, and you were not even allowed to order a drink in any downtown bar without a hat on. (This even applied to the BBC Wales executive producer, who decided for the week in Cheyenne that she should be called Sue – Teleri hardly being a suitable name . . .)

However, despite the hard drinking, there was very little real trouble and folk were right neighbourly. One night, when I ordered a drink (Red Eye naturally), the barman asked where I was from. I told him. He asked me what I did. I squinted my eyes and said, Clint Eastwood fashion, 'I'm a bull rider.'

He looked at me and said slowly, 'Bullshit . . .'

My first day at the rodeo I was introduced to some of the clowns, including a 'barrel man' by the name of Quail Dobbs.

It was explained to me that a 'barrel man' was more of an entertainer than the bull-fighting clowns, and I was to be made up as one.

Quail replaced my laughter lines with 'crow's feet', and fitted me with baggy pants, braces and a floppy hat. The barrel man, Quail, explained he was usually a funny old man built like a fire hydrant who jumped in and out of a padded steel barrel to entertain the crowd, and then braced himself inside it, curled up against the sides, while the bull tilted at it.

After a few disastrous attempts at jumping into the barrel 'butt' first, I managed it and looked forward with some excitement to my first day in the arena.

The other clowns were bull-fighting clowns, whose function it was to keep the bull away from the fallen rider. They were also there in case the barrel should be knocked over and the open end left exposed to the bull's flying hooves and horns. Apparently, there had been cases where bulls had struck their horns into open-ended barrels – seriously injuring the barrel men.

This had not occurred to me . . . I was suddenly glad my smile was freshly painted and I couldn't help thinking . . .

> I shouldn't be here
> In this dusty arena.
> Folks, I ain't all what you see
> 'Cos inside I'm shaking
> With this chance that I'm taking –
> This smile is just painted on me.
>
> No, I shouldn't be here
> In this dusty arena
> With a smile from a tin on a shelf,
> 'Cos though fortune's beguiling
> It's the paint that is smiling –
> I'm none too happy myself . . .

THE BULL-FIGHTING RODEO CLOWN

(Chorus)
The bull-fighting rodeo clown,
He travels to each Rodeo town
To be by your side when you're taking your ride,
The bull-fighting rodeo clown.

Now I've come to Wyoming to the town of Cheyenne,
Just another young cowboy to learn all I can,
To hear all the stories they tell in this town
Of the bull-fighter barrel man rodeo clown.

Now I watched a young cowboy 'fore he got on his ride
Tighten the rope on a Brahma bull's hide.
I watched him get thrown and his 'butt' hit the ground,
But the clown saved his life when he turned the bull round.

In their baggy old trousers, with their smiles and their
    jokes,
They greasepaint the day for the kids and their folks,
They brighten the dusty old frontier town,
The bull-fighting barrel man rodeo clowns.

Now a cowboy don't say much – it isn't his way –
Though the clown lays his life on the line every day
In every performance at each rodeo,
And he does it for cowboys he don't even know.

The bull-fighting rodeo clown,
He'll travel to reach rodeo town
To be by your side when there's nowhere to ride,
He's the bull-fighting rodeo clown.

My manager, Stuart Littlewood, who had just arrived
from England that morning and had never seen a rodeo, was
somewhat taken aback to see those great two-ton Brahma
bulls driven into the bucking chutes and his 'act' climbing
into a barrel. He immediately left the arena and telephoned
an insurance agent in Manchester (at three in the morning)
to double my life insurance.

This in itself filled me with confidence, and I began to feel
a little nervous about being in the confines of the barrel,
especially as I'd heard the bull-fighters admit they wouldn't
entertain it . . . 'If he sticks a horn in there . . .'

I was announced to the crowd over the tannoy and
received a sympathetic round of applause. I jumped into the
barrel and waited for the first bull to be released from the
chutes. The tannoy crackled once more and echoed around
the great arena:

'Wearing 151 . . . riding Moonstone – Brad Johnston.'

The barrel suddenly seemed much nearer the chutes and
I hoped Stuart had managed to get through to England and
to Manchester.

The bull turned out of Chute Three. He was a huge black Brahma with saliva streaming from his mouth and one broken horn hanging loosely at the side of his enormous head. The cowboy rode him well out of the chute but as the bull turned back to the left he kicked and twisted and bucked the young cowboy clear. The bull-fighting clowns moved in to protect the fallen rider, and he scrambled clear. I watched with horror as the bull then turned towards me. I shot down into the safety of the barrel and curled myself tightly against its sides bracing myself for the impact . . . There was none. The bull had run harmlessly past and was being herded in by the outriders back to the bull-pens.

'Okay, Max,' shouted the bull-fighting clowns. The tannoy crackled once more:

'Wearing number 253 . . . riding Lollipop – Randy Dwight.'

I began to relax and enjoy this 'close encounter', and was disappointed to be relieved by Quail after six bulls had been run and only one of them, disappointingly, had tilted at the barrel. For me it had been a bit of an anti-climax, but it had been a great opportunity to observe at close quarters the skills and courage of both rider and clown and the enormous, frightening power of these huge wild bulls.

Later that day I was discussing the day's filming with the director and the film crew outside the arena. I was still in my clown's clothes and said it was a pity, for the sake of the film, that I hadn't been hit harder when I was in the barrel.

As I was still speaking, people began screaming, clutching their children and running in all directions. 'Bull! Bull!' someone shouted hysterically. A huge Brahma had made an apparently impossible leap over the arena fence and was running amuck outside the stadium.

People were falling over themselves in blind panic trying to get out of the path of the rampaging animal. I sought safety on top of a small caravan and watched three cowboys on horseback chasing the bull and attempting to lasso its back legs. They finally succeeded, and the terrified animal was led wild-eyed back to the pens.

The next thing I saw was one of our film crew waving frantically for help and shouting, 'Get an ambulance!'

Our production assistant, 53-year-old Brenda Thomas, had been hit by the bull and was lying crumpled on the ground in an obvious state of shock. An ambulance arrived and Brenda was rushed to hospital, where they later informed us she had suspected broken ribs, heavy bruising, and had narrowly missed being killed.

My Heroes Have Always Been Cowboys

The week following Cheyenne saw me teaming up with a bull rider by the name of Tommy Keith. I was to 'travel down the road' with him, gaining experience of the rodeo circuit before riding myself in my first big competition: the 'Pikes Peak or Bust' Rodeo in Colorado Springs.

In the run-up to my first appearance in rodeo competition it was decided for the purpose of the film to create a 'dream sequence'. I would be seen to be dreaming before my first competitive ride, and my fears and anxieties could manifest themselves in the dream.

I was to appear as an old bull rider turned mountain man who lived alone above the timber line in the Rocky Mountains above Colorado. We hired bear skins, a racoon hat, moccasins and a bowie knife, and I lived the part for the days leading up to shooting the film. I used to check into hotels and the receptionist would say, 'Good evening and welcome to the Holiday Inn. Can I have your name, sir?'

I'd reply in a slow 'Jim Hardy' accent, 'I ain't got no name, but some folks call me Colorado . . .'

I had written a song called 'Colorado' to accompany the film, and one of the verses went:

He was raised above the timber line, where nothing ever
  grows,
But he was the only man alive who could ride old 'Crooked
  Nose'.
He fished the mountain's clear streams . . .

The director decided he liked the song, and because of
the storyline in the lyric he would film me fishing just below
the timber line in the mountains above Colorado.

The only problem was that we had no tackle, and there
could be no guarantee we would catch anything even if we
had. It was therefore decided to buy some trout from a
nearby restaurant and simulate the sequence of actually
catching the fish.

We drove as far as we could along the twisting mountain
road and then dragged all the heavy film equipment up the
last few thousand feet to the lake of the summit. There was
very little oxygen at this height, and we were all exhausted
from the climb. We quickly set up for the sequence, with
the director irritably hurrying us along because of the fading
light.

'Max, go and unpack the trout and tie one on the end of
this line . . . we're losing the light.'

I hurried to open the box and couldn't believe what I saw:
the fish were *filleted*. We had no other option, however, but
to carry on the best we could. We tried to keep the trout
from 'opening out' by tying string around them, muddied so
as not to show. We then filmed 'He fished the mountain's
clear streams . . .'

We tried take after take of Colorado catching trout. It
was absolutely hysterical as the first trout opened out on
entry, the string snapped on the second one, and the third
one broke in half and fell in.

The director, who was shouting at everybody by now and
wringing his hands in despair, was finally happy with Take
Twenty-Seven and I was covered in fish scales.

All this had been watched with growing interest by some

other fishermen away on the other side of the lake, who were astounded at my good fortune and unconventional methods. They hadn't seen a fish rise all day, yet they had seem me land over twenty rainbow trout in as many minutes. Eventually curiosity got the better of them and they wandered over.

'Hi, there,' called this big Texan with all the gear imaginable strapped on him.

'Hey, I've been watching you – you're some fisherman. What's your name, son?'

I looked up and said, 'I ain't got no name but some folks call me Colorado.'

'Pleased to meet you, Colorado. Tell me what you are using for bait.'

I looked up, narrowed my eyes and said slowly, 'Just some old filleted rainbow . . .'

He blinked and said to his friend, 'Well, I'll be darned, I ain't heard o' that before.'

By now we'd lost the light and headed back down the mountain to drive to Colorado Springs, where I was to meet up again with the two bull riders, Tommy Keith and Brian.

While I had been away they had travelled thousands of miles, sometimes competing in rodeos as much as five hundred miles apart in the same day. I had experienced some of this lifestyle the week before, and tried to capture it in a song called 'This is the Life of a Rodeo Cowboy':

THIS IS THE LIFE OF A RODEO COWBOY

Well, he'll wake up on some morning
In towns where he's a stranger,
In places where his stories and his songs don't seem to
   rhyme,
Where folk don't seem to miss him
And others just dismiss him
As just another cowboy, out of place and out of time.

But there's no burning daylight, it's time that he was
    leaving –
No time for hanging pictures, no time to loose the rein,
But he'll stop and ask a friend what he scored last night in
    Denver,
Grab a cup of coffee, then he's on the road again.

Sometimes he might win some, sometimes he'll get lucky,
Sometimes every cowboy has to learn to ride with pain,
But something deep inside him says 'Cowboy, you can ride
    him,'
And the hurt'll sit beside him when he's on the road again.

Sometimes he gets lonely and gets to thinking only
Of the ride he's got tomorrow – will he ever win again?
And his girl she thinks about him, in the time that she's
    without him,
And has she cause to doubt him when he's on the road
    again?

Chorus:
But his is the life of a rodeo cowboy,
This is the life, they say,
In a pair of faded jeans
And a rigging bag of dreams,
Travelling through the night to his eight-second day.

Pikes Peak or Bust

The next day, however, was to be my greatest test. The
Pikes Peak or Bust Rodeo was the next biggest to the
Cheyenne Frontier Days, and I began to get concerned

about riding in actual competition, especially as Brian had told me that at least ten cowboys were killed riding bulls in competition the year before. He made me go cold all over when he described how two of his best friends had died and how he himself had got a bull's horn in his eye. One friend, he said, was stepped on and died instantly, and the other was run through by a long-horn. He described in detail how this young bull rider had then crawled back into the bucking chute to die, driven on by the adrenalin pumping in his already dead body.

I asked him why and how he could go on – after seeing his best friend die like that. 'At first I wanted to quit,' he said, 'and then it was as if Pete was telling me to carry on. He always used to wear a straw hat with a red bandanna and sometimes before I ride now I look up the stands and I swear I can see that 'straw'. I look again, and it's gone. I know he's up there some place and as to your question why I'm still riding? the answer is – *for the both of us, I guess.*'

We continued in silence after that. There was nothing more to say.

To Tommy rodeo was America's *truest* sport, partly because it had its origins way back in the pioneer days. It had been inherited from cowboys who had herded cattle on the great drives through the dusty frontier lands, and whose only break from tedium was to pit their skill and craft against other outfits and other cowboys. Men like Tommy were part of a long tradition, and though sometimes they were 'out of place and out of time', they were proud to belong to a great heritage, and I was proud to have briefly touched it.

When we got to the rodeo the three of us sensed something was wrong. There was a silence and a lack of urgency about everything and everybody. Then we heard that in the opening event a 17-year-old girl had been thrown into a fence and killed.

Despite the terrible tragedy the organising committee

decided the rodeo should carry on. In a rather subdued atmosphere at first, the steer wrestling, calf roping, bare-back and saddle-borne competitions took place. I watched without interest some of the rides and waited impatiently for the 'tour de force', the bull riding. This competition was always kept until last, to ensure that the crowd stayed on until the end of the rodeo day. The crowd buzzed with expectancy and I began to loosen up and do the stretching exercises I had been taught. I paid my entrance fee and shuddered when I heard the name of the bull I had drawn – he was called Bonecrusher. I swallowed hard and went to see him in the pens behind the chute. He was a lean, dark brown animal with long horns. I tried to look unconcerned, but my apprehension registered with Tommy, who took me to one side and said: 'It's OK, Max, I rode him once in Boulder. He ain't nothing special, he turns to the left and bucks a bit, that's all. You don't want any old corn husker from Arkansas your kids could ride. You won't win no silver buckles that way.'

We returned to the chute area and I began to get ready. I was the next but one to be announced, and I strove to prepare myself mentally for the ride. I was desperately anxious to do well and strode impatiently and nervously up and down the area behind the bucking chutes while Tommy prepared my rope. While I was going through these mental processes I heard a voice behind and someone tapping my shoulder. 'Hello, Max. I'm from Ammanford. How's it going?'

It was a man from South Wales who was on holiday in Colorado and had come to the rodeo for the day and read my story in the local paper. Normally I would have been glad to see him and made him feel welcome, but at that moment I needed to be alone with my thoughts – to concentrate on my ride. However, he went on: 'I think you know my Auntie Olwen . . . she used to work with you in the Metal Box . . . she was a checker on 'C' line . . . she says that . . .'

The tannoy crackled into life: 'Ladies and Gentlemen, the

next rider out of Chute Number Four is Max Boyce. A month ago he hadn't ridden a horse, and now he's a bull rider. He's gonna be riding a mean son of a bitch by the name of Bonecrusher.'

I lowered myself down on to the bull, and Tommy adjusted my rope, offering advice at the same time. His voice was urgent now. 'Remember to keep your chin tucked in, Max. We won't let you go till you're good and ready.'

The announcer spoke again: 'Max has come all the way across the water from over there in England.'

'Wales!' yelled a voice from Ammanford. 'My Auntie Olwen . . .'

'It's his first ride in competition here in the Pikes Peak or Bust Rodeo – we wish him well. Let's hear it for Max Boyce.'

I waited nervously for the bull to be in the right position . . . and nodded.

The gate was hauled open and the bull turned quickly to the right, and once again I was instantly and acutely aware of the enormous surging power of these animals. I was terribly nervous, but coldly determined to hang on. I managed somehow to survive the first few crucial seconds without mishap, but then he bucked and turned hard back to his left, throwing me off balance.

The sudden weight transference caused the rope to slip, which left me hanging on perilously down one side, and with each twist and turn of the bull the rope slipped even further. I was now virtually upside down and becoming horribly aware of the bull's flying hooves. Only some basic primeval survival instinct kept me from being thrown.

I desperately tried to cling on but my weight became too much and I was forced to release the rope. As I fell from the side of the bull his hind legs caught me in the small of my back. A last contemptuous gesture.

The next thing I remember was the bull-fighting clowns sweeping the dust off me with a cane-brush and saying, 'Great ride, Max. You didn't tell us you was a trick-rider . . .'

I walked to the edge of the arena, my mind still racing, and tried to relive the ride. In all the noise and excitement I had not heard the buzzer and hadn't realised, until the other bull riders told me, that I had managed an eight-second ride.

I waited with the other bull riders for the marks to be read out.

'Before we have the wild horse race, here are the marks for the bull riding. Tommy Keith – 89 points.'

The crowd roared their approval.

'Clinton Husky – 75. Steve Whittle – 92. Local boy from here in Colorado Springs, Pete Brady – 95 points.'

The crowd erupted.

'And Max Boyce, who made us all laugh, 14 points.'

I knew my ride had been somewhat ungainly, but 14 . . .

Apparently the judges marked for the style of the ride and not for the duration. I had come a creditable last. I was a little disappointed, but so thrilled I had managed to stay with Bonecrusher for eight whole precious seconds.

The cowboys were genuinely pleased for me and shook my hand warmly.

'Well done, Max, you had enough want-to to make it. You did all right.'

Then came another familiar voice: 'Hello, Max! Remember me – I'm from Ammanford. You used to work with my Auntie Olwen . . .'

I laughed and hugged him and told him his Auntie Olwen was the most wonderful woman in the whole world.

We left Colorado the next morning and said our fond farewells to the cowboys and clowns who had helped and cared for me. They were some of the most genuine people I have ever met. They were warm and friendly, honest and caring, and left a deep and lasting impression on me.

Pioneers and Pinnochio

*A*fter we'd finished the Dallas Cowboys film, we started work on another for the Welsh television channel, S4C.

It was to be made in California and told the story of Welsh people who had gone west in search of a new beginning, as their pioneering grandfathers had done before them.

The first place we visited was a Welsh chapel which turned out to be an old Jewish synagogue in the Mexican quarter of Los Angeles. We were introduced to the minister, who was Irish, and he told us that 'John-Boy' of *The Waltons* worshipped there and was learning to speak Welsh. He was of Welsh descent, but unfortunately was away filming in New York.

A few weeks previously, there had been quite astonishing scenes at the chapel, which in many ways summed up life in this part of America.

In the middle of the morning service, hooded gunmen burst into the chapel and threatened to shoot anybody who moved. They instructed each member of the congregation to remove their valuables and turn out their pockets.

One woman, although fearing for her life, pretended to kneel in prayer, and put her rings in her mouth. Unfortunately, when she was bundled against the wall to be searched, she accidentally swallowed them. Her husband never totally forgave her, but in the shy quiet moments, he admits, 'The sun shines out of her . . .'

When the gunmen broke in at the rear of the chapel, they stumbled across the organist, who was preparing his music for the service. He was overpowered, gagged and bound.

In all the confusion, no one noticed he was missing until the following Sunday, when the first hymn was read out . . .

While we were in California, we were invited to stay on the *Queen Mary*, the once proud liner that crossed the Atlantic over a thousand times. It had now sadly been turned into a floating hotel, fulfilling America's need to buy tradition and history.

In attempting to make it even more realistic they had imported London black taxis and double-decker buses to stand awkwardly on the quay. Even more out of place were two 'four-foot' London policemen, who patrolled the area and who answered to the names of Duane and Troy. One lonely Beefeater meanwhile sold hotdogs from a sentry box.

For the purpose of the film we also visited Disneyworld – the children's fantasy land where no one knew where the queue for *Space Mountain* began and the one for *Pirates of the Caribbean* ended.

As we were making a film, we were allowed to go behind the scenes. This, however, resulted in many of my childhood illusions being shattered. There, in the staff canteen, was 'Snow White' in all her purity – smoking.

It was hard to believe that these wonderful characters that were so much part of my childhood were actors and actresses, such was the magical atmosphere created by the Disney dream.

Worse was to follow, however, when I stood next to 'Pinocchio' in the gents' toilet and realised he wasn't made of wood at all . . .

The saddest moment of all came as we were leaving. That was when, after a little difference of opinion, I heard 'Goofy' telling 'Bambi' to 'P. . . off.'

Where's Your Spring Onion?

*T*he leek that has been my constant and closest companion over the years has also been something of a cross to bear and has led to some awkward and hilarious situations.

Two days before we were due to fly to Hong Kong it was being repainted when a workshop van reversed into it and snapped it in half. The leek is made of fibre-glass and someone suggested the only place to have it repaired would be a boat builder. We rang up a firm in Manchester called Fibre Hull Ltd. An Indian voice answered: 'Fibre Hull Limited. What is it, please?'

I explained who I was, hoping he might know of me. He seemed to understand, so I carried on.

'I've got a nine-foot fibre-glass leek that needs repairing.'

'That is no problem, sir, we can fix it. Where is it, please?'

'It's in the lighting truck in Oldham.'

'I'm sorry, we do not repair vehicles, only vessels.'

'No! No!' I laughed. 'You don't understand. It's a . . . leek . . . like you find in the garden – but it's a big fibre-glass one.'

'I'm sorry, sir, but if you have a leak in the garden, surely you are needing a plumber and some alkathene piping. We are only boat builders and repairers.'

I eventually got him to agree to look at it. We took it round in the truck and dragged it into their workshop. They looked at it for a long time and said, 'It will never sail.'

After the mishap in Manchester we decided to have the leek made in two separate sections which could be slotted together. The joint would be covered with a black 'mourning' band symbolising a Welsh rugby defeat.

We also had a steel flight case made to carry it and protect it from uncaring baggage handlers and skis on airport conveyors. The box also came in handy to carry merchandising. We stuffed it full of little four-inch leeks to give away in our Far East concerts. They were made from green and white cloth with two little beady eyes, woollen roots and a red and white scarf tied round their middle. They were primarily to give to children as souvenirs.

All this seemed to us fairly normal but it's not easy explaining it all at three in the morning to a Chinese immigration official at Hong Kong airport who hardly speaks English.

We arrived bleary-eyed after a long-delayed flight from London. Because of past experiences with touring bands and musicians, the airport officials subjected our gear to close scrutiny. They examined our guitars for drugs and then demanded to know what was in the steel box.

I said, 'There's one big leek and about two hundred little leeks.'

They assumed (like the boat builders) that the box had once contained liquid.

'You lose all your water?'

'No,' I said, remembering my experiences with the boat builder. 'They're leeks – you know, the vegetable.'

'You have vegetables in the box?'

'Yes . . . but . . .'

'No vegetable allowed.'

I remonstrated with him. 'It's a fibre-glass vegetable, it's nine-foot long, and the other little ones are woollen.'

He looked at me strangely. 'You have nine-foot glass vegetable?'

Stuart, who had been organising the transport to the hotel but had now returned, was becoming more and more irritated with the delay in clearing customs and the fact that they wanted to break the leek open. He took one airport customs official aside and said, 'Listen, pal, it's a big bamboo shoot – right? He takes it on stage and sings with it.'

I dread to think what they thought I did, but we

eventually got away without having to rip the leek apart. However, I did wonder what the rugby supporters on their way to the Hong Kong Rugby Sevens would make of all the Chinese customs men wearing little leeks . . .

I was whisked away from the airport as we were running late for an interview on the *South China Today* programme (which was in Chinese). I was interviewed by a beautiful young Chinese girl who told me beforehand through an interpreter that she was surprised to find I was white. Apparently she had worked on a Japanese cartoon film called *Arthur and the Britons*. In this film the English are depicted as being a white, warring race who have tanks and guns and who are at constant war with the Welsh, who only have bows and arrows and are all black. She went on to ask me how much truth was there in this film, and had I seen it. I told her I hadn't seen it, but from what she had said it seemed pretty factual, although because of interbreeding some of us were now white . . .

No doubt 'the Welsh are a dark-skinned race' lost a little in the translation. When the time came for her to interview me, I wasn't in the least surprised to be asked: 'Where's your spring onion . . . ?'

A Concert in Hong Kong

*O*ur first concert in Hong Kong was held on the eve of the Hong Kong Invitation Rugby Sevens and was organised by two ex-teachers who ran a company called Clodhoppers Anonymous.

On the morning of the concert I went to see the hall with Rick, my long-serving sound engineer, and we came across some Chinese 'humpers' who were carrying our sound equipment into the theatre up a long steep ramp. The Chinese were very old and painfully thin. They looked much too frail and ill to be doing such work. Rick and I naturally stopped to give them a hand as they staggered under the weight of our equipment, and immediately found ourselves in the middle of an industrial dispute. Apparently for us to help them was an indication that we doubted their ability, their capability – even their manhood. We had inadvertently insulted them.

Stuart Littlewood, my manager, who was co-promoting the tour, handled it in his own inimitable way. He stuffed a bundle of yen into the withered hand of this old Chinese foreman and, pointing at us, said to him: 'They don't understand union procedure.'

The old man blinked and shuffled back to work. The whole exercise had cost us thirty pounds: ten pounds for them to lift the gear, and twenty pounds for us to help them.

'You've got to understand these people,' said Stuart (from Oldham).

'You've got to talk their language.'

Steve 'Mostyn' Evans

We had further problems of communication during the actual concert. The technical staff in charge of the lighting were naturally all Chinese and spoke no English whatsoever. It would not have mattered a great deal apart from the fact that in my stage act there were several lighting effects which included dry ice and a smoke machine. These effects were cued by certain words and sentences written out for the lighting operator (which when you're Chinese are very difficult to understand).

Because of Stuart's success with the 'humpers', he was called on to sit in as an 'interpreter' to supervise and cue all the special effects.

'I can handle it,' says Stuart.

However, it proved more difficult than he'd imagined, for Chinese is very different to English and some words and sentences take longer to say in Chinese than they do in English.

I got to the part in the concert where I did a parody on the *Six Million Dollar Man* which involved special lighting and a stroboscope to simulate Steve 'Mostyn' Evans running in slow motion. I began to tell the story:

'Steve "Mostyn" Evans – rugby player, a man barely alive. Gentlemen, we can rebuild him. We have the technology, we have the capability to make the world's first bionic Number Eight. Steve "Mostyn" Evans will be that man, better than he was before. Better even than Mervyn Davies was: better, stronger, faster.'

This was the cue to operate the strobe, the special lighting and the theme music from the *Six Million Dollar Man*. Stuart, who had followed the lines religiously, spoke into his walkie-talkie which linked him to the interpreter.

'Cue strobe . . .'

The interpreter then spoke to the operator.

'O light that shines from within and is brighter than six suns and two moons and caresses my eyes with a fountain of seeing . . .'

'Cue strobe,' screams Stuart through the intercom, seeing me trying to run in slow motion . . . in bright light, centre stage. Still seeing no reaction, and with time running out, Stuart clambers into the lighting box, throws a switch . . . and inadvertently operates the smoke machine!

Steve 'Mostyn' Evans is now engulfed in smoke. The band are on their knees laughing when someone shouts from the audience, 'He's blown a fuse, Max.'

Despite this mishap (which was the funniest part of the show) it was a great success, and for me it was a great thrill to play in front of fifteen hundred people in Hong Kong – despite the counter-attraction of Elton John who was 'in concert' in Hong Kong on the same night. I used this in the concert by saying,

'I understand Barry John's elder brother is playing down the road and has sold out the stadium. Barry got capped but I always thought Elton was the more talented . . .'

As we left the theatre after the concert we passed the same Chinese 'humpers' loading up the gear. They recognised us and Stuart and, with bony hands outstretched, asked invitingly,

'You help . . . You help?'

'You can p . . . off,' said Stuart.

Rick chipped in unmercifully, 'Now, now, Stuart, you've got to understand these people . . .'

'Bellows'

The international rugby sevens in Hong Kong were unlike any competition I had seen, and I thrilled at the prospect of watching the Japanese play New Zealand and Korea play France.

The atmosphere at the ground was carnival-like, and whoever was playing, the crowd always supported the underdog. The Australian side came in for some terrible, though good-natured abuse from the crowd for taking it all too seriously.

Each side naturally had its supporters, but none more colourful than the Bahrain side. Nearly all British 'ex-pats', they were dressed in Arab national costume and prayed to Allah they wouldn't draw the Aussies in the first round.

The New Zealand supporters had, it seemed, bought Hong Kong out of gravy browning, spears and grass skirts, and stuck their tongues out at everybody in traditional Maori greeting.

Union Jacks mixed with the green of Ireland, while the Australian supporters bought dry martinis with cherries for the Scottish lads in kilts, and the Japanese bowed to all and sundry.

Amongst all this colour and good humour was one band of loyal supporters who stood out, musically, head and shoulders above the rest: a splinter-group of . . . the Hong Kong Welsh Male Voice Choir.

They were resplendent in red and white shirts and sat near the halfway line supporting Crawshay's Seven (almost entirely made up of Welsh players). Though not at full strength, the choir had their conductor with them (dressed in tails, naturally) and even more remarkable was the fact that they had . . . *a piano in the stand*!

Actually it was an organ, and required two people to operate it – the organist, Dai 'Owain' Price (LRAM), and, just as important, a man who supplied air to the organ. This he did personally by blowing into a thick rubber tube connected to the organ. His name was Ben Davies, but he was affectionately known as 'Bellows' and was an integral part of the choir, having blown in many such important outdoor events, including at least one Eisteddfod and an ox-roasting.

As Crawshay's Seven took the field, led by Clive Rees of London Welsh, the conductor rapped his baton on the side of the stand, called his choir to order and announced the first piece of music, *Comrades in Arms*.

This stirring work takes some singing and I have heard great choirs struggling with the difficult middle sections. Not so the splinter-group of the Hong Kong Welsh Male Voice Choir – they sang magnificently.

As the game neared its exciting conclusion the conductor announced that they would sing the Slaves' Chorus from *Nabucco*.

> Speed thy journey,
> My thoughts and my longings,
> Speed thy journey o'er mountain and valley . . .

Unfortunately, because of the exciting nature of the game, the crowd noise had risen in volume and the second tenors complained that they couldn't hear the organ.

'More air,' shouted the conductor, 'More air!' Ben's face was purple, his cheeks like two Ogen melons, the veins on his neck standing out like haulage ropes. The choir sang, appropriately:

> O inspire us, Jehovah, with courage,
> So that we may endure to the last,
> So that we . . .

The Crawshay's Seven were now only a point behind, with a scrummage in front of the American Eagles' posts. The crowd noise was deafening.

'More air,' pleaded the organist. 'More air!'

I swear the people all around Ben Davies loosened any tight clothing as they struggled for air themselves, while 'Bellows' took great gulps of sky in an attempt to maintain the organ's tone and sound.

When, mercifully, the final whistle blew, leaving the Crawshay's Seven the narrow winners, Ben collapsed. The air rushed out of the organ, lowering its tone and sending the whole first bass out of tune.

Ben Davies was rushed to the First Aid tent and examined by the Irish Wolfhounds' team doctor who enquired whether he had been *playing*, to get into this exhausted condition?

'No,' said one of the choristers who had carried him there.

'Dai Price was playing – Ben was only blowing.'

Which Room Are You In, Sir?

*O*ne of the drawbacks of touring is the amount of time spent in hotels. On the whole they have been hospitable and friendly, but there have been exceptions.

In one hotel, after noticing they had lamb on the menu, I innocently asked the waiter, 'Is it Welsh?'

He replied curtly, 'Do you want to talk to it or eat it?'

Then there was the time in New Zealand in 1980 when we stayed in the same hotel as we had in 1978.

I walked up to the packed public bar and again wanting to appear friendly, said to the harrassed barman, 'I came in here about two years ago.'

He looked up and said, 'Jesus, I'm serving as fast as I can.'

My most memorable story concerning hotels, however, happened in Sydney, in a hotel near the El Alamein fountain in King's Cross. We were checking into reception when a drunken Irishman staggered down the stairs and said to the young receptionist, 'I want to change my room.'

'What room are you in, sir?' enquired the young girl.

'254.'

'But sir, that's the best room in the hotel, it's got a private bar and a jacuzzi, a four-poster bed and a beautiful view of Sydney Harbour bridge and the famous Opera House.'

'I want to change my room,' he insisted.

'I'm new here,' explained the receptionist, 'I'll have to speak to the manager.'

The manager duly arrived and asked in a pin-striped voice, 'What seems to be the trouble, sir?'

'I want to change my room.'

'That shouldn't be a problem, we're not full tonight, what room are you in?'

'254.'

'But sir, that's the best room in the hotel, it's got . . .'

'I know what you're going to say,' interrupted the Irishman. 'It's got the fancy bath and the bar and the view of the bridge and . . .'

'Then why do you want to change it?'

The Irishman drew himself to his full height and said, 'It's on fire . . .'

More Kitchen Cloths and Fan Belts

*M*y last tour of the Middle East was a very extensive one, taking in Abu Dhabi, Doah in Qatar, Al Ain, Bahrain, Dubai and Dukan.

Abu Dhabi has always sounded to me like a disease. I can imagine anxious parents waiting in a hospital and a grave-faced doctor confronting them.

The father asks, 'Is it serious, Doctor?'

'I'm afraid so. It's . . . Abu Dhabi.'

'Oh no!'

In Qatar we experienced for the first time the strict no drinking laws of the Moslem faith. The band prepared themselves for the dry week in the same way as a camel does. They were suitably fortified the night before we flew. The airport at Doah was an extremely unfriendly, hostile place and we all felt distinctly wary.

The organisers of the concert, the Doah players, were however great folk and the little theatre they had built themselves was a credit to them. After a memorable concert, with fruit juices served during the interval, we were all invited back to the house for one of the organisers for refreshments. Our bass player, Joe Fagin of *Auf Wiedersehen Pet* fame, sat in a flowery armchair having serious withdrawal symptoms when a tall, stiff lady approached him.

'Tea?'

Joe winced, but out of politeness answered somewhat shakily, 'Yes please.'

She smiled knowingly and poured him a large cup out of an old china teapot.

He sipped at it and then a smile lit up his face. It was lager!

'Another cup?' asked the tall, stiff lady.

'I'm afraid I'm a bit of a teapot,' admitted Joe. 'I'd love another cup – no sugar, no milk.'

Skinny Dipping in Al Ain

One of the most unusual concerts we performed was in a place called Al Ain (one of the earliest recorded oases) in the United Arab Emirates.

After the concert I was invited along with a few other people to a party. It was to be given by a very rich, influential Arab sheikh.

I accepted readily and climbed into the back of his

sumptuous Rolls-Royce, which was upholstered in tiger skin, to be chauffeur-driven to his home.

His house turned out to be quite a mansion, with electrically operated gates which security guards opened by remote control.

We made our way up a long drive, flanked by date palms, to the house. Later we sat around the beautiful swimming pool, drinking champagne and listening to traditional Eastern music.

After a little while the Arab owner suggested we all had a swim in the pool. All inhibitions were cast aside and some of the girls stripped off and dived in. They giggled and screamed and dared us to join them in the dark pool.

I watched from a Sunday school distance, occasionally risking one eye while pretending to be totally unconcerned, fidgeting with my glass and making gabbled, meaningless conversation with a BP welder who I'm sure never heard a word I was saying.

After further goading from the pool, I decided to show them my inward two and a half somersault dive in the tucked position (with a 1.6 degree of difficulty). I had started to take my shirt off, hoping I had clean underpants, when the owner took my arm.

'Not you, Mr Boyce. Not you, I have something special for you. Come, I will show.'

He led me to his house, my imagination running wild.

I didn't know what to expect. I had visions of great black men stripped to the waist waving palm fronds; hubble bubble pipes and bejewelled belly dancers; veiled girls bringing me fine wine in gold goblets and feeding me black grapes. I was terribly excited, nervous and filled with apprehension.

The Sheikh opened a great door and ushered me inside a dimly lit room.

'Close your eyes, I have a surprise for you, and do not open them until I say!'

He led me to one end of the room and said, 'Now open them!'

108

I looked up and there it was in front of me – *a dartboard* . . .

I was in a pub. He had built a replica of an English pub in one of the rooms in his house.

It had beer pumps, horse brasses, plastic oak beams and a dartboard, all shipped out from England.

His passion was darts, and he demanded I play with him.

'Come,' he said, 'We play 501 – best of three legs. Here are your arrows.'

Now I have never been a good darts player, and the Sheikh was no better . . . My first dart thudded into a beam, my second missed altogether and the third hit the wire and bounced out. We were nearly an hour getting a double, mainly because of the shrieks and screams coming from the pool.

When we finally left the 'Red Lion', the pool was deserted (apart from dirty underpants). Dawn was breaking, and far away we could hear the prayers to Mecca echoing from the mosques around Al Ain.

When I eventually returned to our hotel the band were having breakfast and they were all eager to hear my story and to ask what happened.

'Where did Ali Baba take you?'

'What have you been doing, you little . . .'

'Playing darts,' I replied.

'You bloody liar,' laughed Rick.

'Why don't you believe me?'

Rick got to his feet, looked at me closely and said, 'There's no chalk behind your ear . . .'

Bahrain

Despite the warm welcome we received all over the Middle East, my most vivid recollection was of a rather sinister religious festival in Bahrain, known as the festival of Ashoora. It was only after much persuasion that I was allowed to witness this remarkable event, and only then accompanied by a local dignitary.

Apparently some hundred years ago a member of a Shiite tribe murdered a religious leader (not for the last time), and the Festival of Ashoora is their day of atonement, an attempt to make up for the sins of their fellow tribesmen.

The narrow, dusty streets were packed with people, and the women and children sat quietly huddled at the side of the road, draped in black from head to foot, and with their faces covered in religious observance. We could hear in the distance a strange thudding sound that echoed down the streets and a rhythmic, primeval chanting. Then into view came a procession led by a camel, also draped in black, with a box-like construction perched on top of its back, symbolising the house of death.

Behind the camel walked the men of the Shiite tribe. I could see from a distance that their hands and arms were crimson red. At first I thought it must be paint, but as they drew nearer I could see it was blood.

A man at the head of the procession chanted a prayer. The others answered while simultaneously beating their bare chests with the palms of their hands. They inhaled deeply, and the chest cavity acted as a drum, producing the deep thudding sound. Driven by this chanting, they proceeded to thrash themselves with chains and knives and sharp implements until they bled freely.

Older men walked alongside casting incense on to the open wounds and praying aloud. Some eventually collapsed in the dusty streets and were carried away while others, bleeding profusely yet seemingly feeling no pain, staggered on. Many of them seemed to be in a state of hypnosis or some kind of religious trance, for they were oblivious to everything and everyone.

We walked back to the hotel in silence, deeply moved by this ceremony. I was acutely aware that I had witnessed another culture and another time. Looking back from 1987, following the recent troubles, it all sounds depressingly familiar.

There's Sand in the Jelly

The last concert in the Middle East was in Dubai. It was planned to coincide with the seven-a-side rugby tournament being held that weekend, with teams from all over the Middle East competing. After the final there was to be a huge barbecue followed by our concert.

Rick O'Brien, my faithful roady, and some hired help, started erecting the stage and sound system first thing in the morning. They had built one side of the stage and the speaker stacks when a violent sandstorm blew up. The wind whipped the sand up into our faces and presented huge problems for everyone: ourselves, the players in the tournament and the caterers who were organising the barbecue. We had to take down our speaker stacks, the rugby tournament was unable to start, and the caterers bravely but vainly tried to keep the sand out of the jelly . . .

We were told that the storm could either last for days or could die down as quickly as it had blown up. In an attempt to cover all eventualities we decided to look for an indoor venue. This, however, proved difficult, and we pondered on the very real possibility of having our last concert in the Middle East cancelled because of a *sandstorm*.

Our beleaguered promoter, Bill Thomson, was now showing signs of panic, taking Valium and facing Mecca while Stuart, my manager, rang his insurance broker in Oldham to ask whether a sandstorm was an 'act of God'.

The Indian caterers were inconsolable, saying to the promoters, 'You are thinking you have problems – they are nothing compared to ours. We have got sand in the jelly . . .'

We hastily arranged a meeting with the tournament organisers who had also co-promoted the concert and made the decision that, whatever happened, in the best tradition of the theatre the show somehow would have to go on.

The secretary of the seven-a-side tournament took me to one side and said, 'See, Max, we're all in the same boat.

We're going to have to play *into it*. You're going to have to sing *through it*, and the caterers will have sand *in it*.'

Mercifully, however, by late afternoon the storm had died down a little and the wind dropped to a level that made it possible to rig up the sound equipment. The band, who had slept through the storm, had by now arrived and the sound check proved that it was possible to sing and be heard. Nevertheless, the sound and lighting equipment was only just adequate and we all realised it was going to be difficult. I was grateful, however, that we didn't have to contend with a full-blown sandstorm.

The audience, largely made up of 'ex-pats', realised we were working under tricky conditions and appreciated our efforts. Thanks to their understanding and fairness it turned out to be a magic night and a fitting climax to our tour.

As I sat in the band's dressing-room afterwards, reminiscing about the last few days, I watched Joe Fagin picking at some prawns left over from the buffet and heard him remark in that lovely lilting Geordie accent, 'The prawns are fresh, you can taste the sand!'

Dukan

One of the remotest places I have visited is the Dukan oil field, eighty miles out in the desert from Doah. It was an extremely inhospitable area, with the temperature well into the hundreds. We lay by this swimming pool in the middle of a building site and John Luce, my bass guitarist, asked, 'Where would we be today now, if we weren't here?' I thought aloud: 'Let's see, what day is it? Saturday – Oh! I know; I'd be in Brecon. Gareth Owen is getting married – I was supposed to go to the wedding.'

'Well, said John, wiping the perspiration from his brow and looking up at the sun beating down from the clear blue sky – 'They've had a lovely day for it anyway . . .'

To the North of Katmandu

$\mathcal{F}$ollowing the success of the American football and rodeo series, Opix Films were always on the lookout for new adventures for me.

The morning before I flew to the Middle East they rang me up at home and asked whether I would be interested in playing polo on elephants. I laughed and didn't take them seriously as I had never even heard of such a game.

It transpired that they had been approached by Cartier, the jewellers, to film the 1985 World Elephant Polo Championship in Nepal and that if certain budgets and fees could be agreed they'd want me to be involved.

I was fascinated by the thought of going to Nepal and agreed on principle. I didn't really think it would ever happen and decided not to think any more of it.

A day before we were due to fly home from the Middle East I had a long phone call from the producer at Opix Films explaining that everything had been agreed and that I was to fly to Delhi and then on to Katmandu as soon as possible. The only problem, the producer explained, was the fact that I needed inoculation against the tropical diseases in the area.

The list was an alarmingly long one:

Yellow Fever
Malaria
Cholera
Typhoid
Tetanus

Luckily a friend of mine living in Dubai arranged for me to have all the necessary injections and I felt as if I was off to fight in Burma with the Chindits. The next morning both my arms were extremely sore and stiff and with a slight fever from the cholera injection nevertheless I had to fly to Delhi to meet up with the film crew and the other members of the Cartier team, who were Billy Connolly, Ringo Starr and his wife Barbara Bach.

Not even in my wildest dreams did I envisage that one day I would be flying to Delhi from the Middle East where I had been inoculated against cholera and yellow fever so that I could play polo on elephants with one of the Beatles.

Delhi

Delhi airport almost defies description. It was quite an incredible scene and I couldn't believe it was an international airport. We waited in the transit area for our luggage. The baggage handling conveyors were quite inadequate, and we watched helplessly through plate glass windows as our cases and equipment disappeared under huge piles of baggage. The whole area was utter chaos.

The situation wasn't helped any by the fact that the two 747s that had landed minutes apart were full of Indian peasants returning from working in the hills. Many of them were carrying all their worldly possessions in cardboard boxes tied with string. Some of these duly burst open, spewing their entire contents over everything. There were mattresses wrapped around television sets and boxes of

114

pomegranates, candles and figs. These split open too, and the contents either rolled away or were trodden on by the people frantically trying to reclaim their baggage from amongst the bedding and the boxes of vegetables.

'Don't worry,' said a little Indian attendant, 'I am going and stopping the conveyor.'

We begged the airport officials to let us through immigration to claim our luggage before it was crushed or lost forever. I explained that we were in transit to Nepal and our flight was being called.

He waved Billy Connolly and myself away, saying, 'I am sorry but your visa is only for Nepal. Your cases are in India.'

Most of us did eventually reclaim our luggage, more through unashamed bribery than persuasion. Billy, sad to say, never saw his suitcase ever again, and I watched him patiently filling out a lost luggage claim and carefully answering all the questions he was being asked.

'What is your occupation please?'

'Flower arranger . . .'

We eventually flew to Katmandu on a small aircraft that would not have looked out of place on an *It Ain't Half Hot Mum* set. However, we landed safely and were driven to our hotel, which was in complete contrast to the simple peasant dwellings we had passed on the way from the airport. Although we had not slept for twenty-four hours, the fascination of Katmandu outweighed our tiredness.

Katmandu

Old Katmandu was built for people not vehicles. Even cycle rickshaws, their rubber bulbed horns stridently tooting, were barely able to negotiate the throng of people crowding the narrow streets. Add to this the babble of tongues, the ringing of bells, the quarrelling of dogs, the chanting of prayers and the twittering of swallows and swifts. We watched them darting to nests beneath the eaves of the houses with intricately carved window frames splitting with age and decay.

It was an overwhelming experience. All one's senses and instincts were involved – including that of survival, since sacred cows and bulls roamed freely in the streets.

It seemed there were almost as many temples as houses, each temple complete with its wind bells, their chimes sounding man's devotion to his gods. We passed a fearsome black figure with six arms and a necklace of severed heads. It was the male consort of the god of destruction, whose wrath could only be placated with animal sacrifice.

A little further on we entered a small courtyard. The Kumari lived here, we were told. The Kumari is a young Newari girl selected to be the Virgin Goddess. The selection committee consists of priests and religious fathers. Likely candidates must first measure up to the thirty-two prescribed 'perfections', which include eyelashes like a cow's, stiff hair growing naturally to the right and a body shaped like a banyan tree. Young girls who possess these pre-requisites are then deliberately shut away in a dark room with recently severed heads from animal sacrifices and frightening noises which combine to shock and frighten the girls.

The new Kumari is easily singled out as the one who does not cry out or show signs of fear. Once discovered, the Virgin Goddess is taken to her residence where she remains until she sheds blood from a cut or from menstruation, thus showing herself to be only human.

I walked through the narrow crowded streets, rubbing shoulders with lamas and garlanded cows and inhaling smoke from incense sticks and butter lamps.

We were all enthralled and I longed to know more of their culture, traditions and history. The Nepalese people were gentle, smiling and friendly and had a wonderful religious tolerance towards each other. Buddhists worshipped freely at Hindu shrines. Then there were the children tugging shyly at our sleeves selling their little trinkets.

'Only one rupee . . . only one.'

I found it impossible to refuse them. The bangles and bracelets were hammered out of copper wire and brass. Our self-appointed guide, a young Nepalese boy, explained that I had bought enough bangles to ensure the telephone linesmen of Nepal would be working over the weekend. That evening, when I tried to ring home and repeatedly failed to get through, I realised why my only contact with the outside world was not working . . . I was wearing it.

We were sorry we had to leave this fascinating place, with its noise and bustle, its powder-sprinkled idols, where white was the colour of mourning, but we knew we could never see everything, no matter how long we stayed.

Elephant Polo

Leaving Katmandu, we journeyed by Land Rover, through some of the wildest country I have ever seen, to the Tiger Tops jungle lodge, some fifty miles away in the Chitwan National Park. We followed the twisting mountain road through the terraced rice fields that were stepped into the hillside.

Set against the magnificent backdrop of the Himalayan Mountain Range, they reminded me of a great empty concert hall.

On the way we passed the simple peasant villages. They were undoubtedly the most primitive I have ever seen, but all the doorways were hung with offerings to the gods Vishnu and Shiva. However, the people and especially the children appeared so happy and ran out to us waving and smiling and calling, 'Bye Bye. Bye Bye,' – apparently the only English word they know.

I watched them and marvelled at their inventiveness and the little games they played – one with berries and stones, and another where a piece of ripped tyre off a Land Rover became a ball, with cardboard as their bat.

I couldn't help but think, reflecting on their simple but seemingly so happy way of life, that *I was poorer by far*.

WITH A ROUND STONE AND A JAR

On a mountain's empty concert hall,
I sat amongst the stalls
And wondered at this unspoilt land
Where the wild Trisuli sprawls,
And I watched the tinsled buses
Winding through the afternoon
As the lines of silver paper
Sang an offering to the Moon.

And I heard the wind-bells' tinkling song
Played by the kindly breeze
And the prayer flags' gentle flutter
In a vain attempt to please,
And I longed to know these people's thoughts
As I watched them shyly stare
And wondered at this different faith
I found too late to share.

We rode on down that dusty road
Beneath the reddening skies,
And laughed as waving children
Turned hellos into goodbyes,
And I watched them play their simple games
With a round stone and a jar,
And I couldn't help but thinking
I was poorer by far.

And I wondered what they dreamt about
By their butter lamps at night
In their humble dwelling places
Where the wind blows out the light.
And did they dream of distant lands
Beyond the furthest star,
Where children play with berries,
A round stone and a jar?

After some four hours' driving we stopped to eat our packed lunch by the sprawling River Trisuli. We sat down on the banks of the river and watched some laughing children splashing and playing in the river. I went to take some photographs and to my horror found the naked body of a woman lying in the river. She had in her mouth a small piece of coal, which our guide explained was a symbolic act of cremation. Her family had cast her body traditionally to the river and because they were too poor to buy the necessary requirements for cremation they symbolised the act with the piece of coal. We were all deeply shocked, but our guide explained that it was not uncommon and to the people of this region death was no stranger.

We had no stomach for eating now, and we abandoned our lunch and drove on to the Chitwan National Park. We finally and thankfully arrived after the sixty-mile journey which had taken us over six hours, during which we were thrown about on the narrow twisting mountain roads with sheer drops on either side.

The jungle lodge was built on stilts and situated in the middle of dense jungle, which we were told was inhabited by several different forms of wild life including tiger, rhino and crocodile. The lodge was very basic, with no electricity and no telephone.

The film crew were put up in tents near the lodge, and as darkness fell and the sounds of the jungle increased, no one slept easy. Every shadowy tree was a rhino, and every rustling sound a man-eating tiger.

Glenda, our production assistant, was not at all happy and was further distressed when she was shown a spider which measured some five inches across. Russ Walker, our cameraman, swore he saw one trying his trousers on . . . Glenda was not amused, and swore she'd never be able to close her eyes, let alone sleep.

The next morning we woke to find the lodge shrouded in mist and heard the laboured sound of the hand driven pump as it clanked water to the few rooms of the jungle lodge.

I showered in freezing cold water, which was luxury compared with the film crew's bucket of water and a bar of green Lifebuoy soap left over from a Gurkha's First World War survival kit.

There were no toilet facilities other than the freedom of the Chitwan National Park. Despite the need for privacy the film crew never ventured far into the steamy jungle, preferring instead to answer the call of nature in a position of safety rather than decency.

We made our way by Land Rover and raft to the elephant polo ground. The raft was made from a hollowed-out tree, and its lowness in the water left us all a little concerned as we had been told the river was infested with crocodiles. Although we had also been told they were only fish eaters no one trailed their fingers in the water for fear the crocodiles might feel like a little change. (Any mishap would have resulted in the original fish finger . . .)

When we landed safely on the other side we had our first view of the elephants. They looked out of the mist like great grey ghosts slowly moving upstream to the polo field.

The mahoots were skilfully driving them, with their bare feet prodding and nudging behind the elephants' ears. The elephants were being taken to have patterns painted on them with coloured chalks, which gave them a startling new appearance.

I looked forward with boyish exuberance to our first game, which was to be against the Gurkhas. They were four commissioned senior officers who would not have looked out of place on the set of *The Jewel in the Crown*. They were friendly, but frightfully Army, and were obviously the last remnants of the Raj. They had of course played elephant polo before, spoke fluent Nepalese and had never lost a game.

We had been given a crash course on the rules of elephant polo, none of which made any sense to Billy, Ringo, Barbara or myself. We decided to play it cavalier fashion and throw caution to the winds. There was to be no game plan, and no elephant to elephant marking.

It soon became evident that the choice of polo sticks was of paramount importance. There were hundreds to choose from, all of different lengths and thicknesses. The slender ones were light but far too whippy, whilst the stiff-shafted ones proved impossible to swing. After much indecision we eventually chose the ones that fitted our elephants and felt most comfortable.

The mahoots instructed the elephants to sit, and we dragged ourselves on behind the mahoots by means of the ropes which served to keep us from falling off and as makeshift stirrups. We were effectively tied on to the elephants, which was just as well, for when they stood up the ground seemed a long way down.

After a few practice runs and tilts the referee, sitting astride a vast African elephant with huge tusks, blew the whistle to begin the first 'chukka'.

Barbara Bach drove her baby elephant forward and squealed her way to the first physical confrontation with the opposition – Brigadier Hunt-Davis of the 7th Gurkha Division. She reached the ball first, took an almighty swing

and missed it by about two feet and nearly fell off. The Brigadier, urged on by his 'chaps', whacked it away from the centre spot and attacked down the left flank. He was doing rather well until his own personal stick was splintered out of his hand by a crushing Ian St Connolly tackle.

'I say, steady on old boy,' snorted the Brigadier.

Billy's answer was lost amongst the trumpeting of the elephants.

In his very first tackle of the World Polo Championships Billy had come close to being sent off and was fortunate to have escaped with only a caution.

The game was never going to be a classic and hardly pleased the connoisseur of elephant polo. Whatever the purist might say, however, there was a great deal of honest effort, much endeavour and intelligent running off the ball by Ringo Starr. Ringo undoubtedly was feeling the effects of an earlier tackle and would have been substituted had we had a substitute. He had what could only be described as an indifferent game and was guilty of a lot of loose play. He made no contact at all with the ball and was severely spoken to by the referee for accidentally whacking one of the opposition's elephants on the trunk. Something that had never been seen before at this level of polo.

Mercifully the whistle went for half-time and, such is the democratic and fair way the game is played, we swapped elephants. This proved our downfall, for elephants never forget, and the elephant Ringo had whacked was never quite the same again and certainly never at ease with Ringo astride him brandishing his stick like a shillelagh. Because of the elephant's understandable reluctance to 'get stuck in' we virtually played the second half with only three elephants.

Billy was magnificent at the heart of our defence and managed to terrify the Brigadier with his Hannibal-like charges, dislodging his stick and his pith helmet on frequent occasions. During a skirmish in front of goal my elephant actually stepped on the ball and buried it. Play was held up for several minutes while the ball was dug out and I was booked for time-wasting and ungentlemanly conduct. This break in play allowed the Gurkhas to regroup and to deploy some of their set-piece moves.

They were helped in no small measure by the fact that Ringo's elephant was fertilising a huge area outside the six-yard box and was unable to continue for several minutes. The Gurkhas inevitably scored and went on to win two-nil.

The world press were unanimous in their condemnation of the Cartier team, and the headlines screamed at us next morning, labelling us as – 'ANIMALS'.

Tiger, Tiger!

We returned to the Tiger Tops lodge, suitably chastened, in the late afternoon. We had just ordered some drinks when a bell rang out and the camp suddenly became a frantic hive of activity. The bell was a signal that a wild tiger had been lured to a part of the jungle where it could be seen and observed. It had been lured there by the staking out of live bait, which seemed cruel but apparently was essential. When the bell rang everyone ran in all directions in a frenzied dash so as not to miss the chance of seeing a tiger in its natural surroundings.

We clambered on to the Land Rovers, which drove part of the way into the jungle, and then we continued on foot. When we got nearer to where the tiger had taken the bait, we were asked in hushed whispers to remove our shoes and continue quietly in absolute and utter silence.

We all linked hands and were led in complete darkness through the dense jungle, not knowing where we were going or what was going to happen. I must admit at this stage I felt distinctly uneasy creeping through the jungle in bare feet, and had it not been for the silence imposed I would have casually said, 'I think I'll go back now – I'm not fussy if I see one or not.' (Later everybody else admitted to feeling the same.)

Suddenly we came into a clearing and were abruptly stopped, bumping into one another in the process amid stifled squeals and frightened giggles. Across the ravine we could see the tiger, lit by a small searchlight, tearing and gnawing at a young water buffalo it had just killed. The tiger was a fully grown male, and although it was a cruel and gruesome sight one couldn't help but marvel at this magnificent wild beast.

Meanwhile, back in the jungle lodge, an even more bizzare scene was being enacted. Steve Strange, the outrageous rock singer, had arrived from England to play in the polo and was sleeping off the effects of alcohol and the long flight, completely oblivious of the practice of baiting tigers and therefore totally unaware of why the bell was ringing. He lay in a deep sleep and wearing only his underpants. Then he was suddenly aware of someone banging on his door shouting excitedly 'Tiger! Tiger!' and people running in all directions.

He leapt to his feet wild-eyed and, naturally, terrified, expecting to see a maneater at the foot of the stairs.

'Tiger! Tiger!' shouted the young native boys. Steve began to run, not knowing from which direction the tiger was coming or where he was going.

'Tiger! Tiger! – quick sir,' pleaded one of the boys. Steve, mistaking the boy's genuine excitement for terror, grabbed hold of the bewildered youngster and fled with him to safety. The boy, not being able to speak English, was astonished to be carried off by this spiky-haired stranger in his underpants.

Steve, in all fairness, was intent on saving both their lives and, so the story goes, ended up on the roof of the jungle lodge with a terrified young Nepalese waiter.

'It's all right now, son,' said Steve, pacifying the boy. 'We'll be safe up here . . .'

On the 7.08 for Swansea

*W*hen I returned home from Nepal we flew into Heathrow Airport and then made our way across London to Paddington Station to catch the 125 high speed train to South Wales. I slumped down in my seat hoping I wouldn't attract too much attention. All I wanted to do was close my eyes and go to sleep.

Just as the train was pulling out of the station I was vaguely aware of someone taking the seat across the way. I half opened my eyes and saw to my surprise, sitting opposite . . . Stuart Burrows, a fellow Welshman and arguably the world's leading lyrical tenor. I was pleased to meet him, but hastened to explain that I was extremely tired and wouldn't be very good company.

Stuart Burrows laughed. 'Don't worry, I feel the same way. We've just finished a week of Verdi's *Otello* at Covent Garden and I'm shattered myself – we'll have a chat in Newport.'

The train trundled through the night and I fell into a deep sleep. It hadn't reached Reading when I felt someone pull at my jacket.

'Max, Max!'

I opened my eyes to find the compartment full of soldiers. The Welsh Regiment were returning from duty in Northern Ireland and had stumbled across me on their way back from the bar in the restaurant car. 'Max, hey Max, give us a song? – Oggie, Oggie, Oggie!'

'Oh,' I said. 'We're on a train, lads, I can't sing on a train, there's people trying to sleep and read.' It was to no avail.

'C'mon mun – give us a song – "Up and under here we go . . ."'

127

I tried to argue but then another soldier thrust a carton of Newcastle Brown on to the table.

'Have a drink with the boys, Max, and give us hymns and arias, c'mon – "And we were singing . . ." '

'Listen,' I said, 'I'll have a drink with you but I don't want to sing, not on a train . . .'

'Only one, Max, – *Sospan Fach* . . . c'mon give us a song, mun?'

Suddenly Stuart Burrows, who had sat quietly through all this, said coldly, 'He's *not* singing.'

The young soldier spun around to face Stuart and demanded, 'Who are you – his manager is it?'

'Yes,' replied Stuart, 'and he's not singing . . . but if you like, I'll sing in his place.'

'We don't want you to sing – we want Max, c'mon *Sospan Fach* – "Yn berwi ar y tan . . ." '

After a while the young soldier, realising I wasn't going to be persuaded, turned to Stuart, poked him with a beer can and said, 'Go on then, you sing.'

Stuart rose slowly to his feet, cleared his throat and sang, 'Waft her angels through the skies.'

Everyone in the carriage was stunned as Stuart's magnificent tenor voice rang through the third carriage of the 7.08 London to Swansea train. Commuters woke from their *Financial Times* and the young soldiers fell quiet and just stood there, as if hypnotised, unable to believe what they were hearing.

After Stuart Burrows had finished, he sat down in absolute silence. The private moved over towards him. Pointing to me he said, 'I don't know much about music, but as far as I'm concerned – you're wasting your time managing him . . .'